SECRET PRESTON

Keith Johnson

AMBERLEY

First published 2015

Amberley Publishing
The Hill, Stroud
Gloucestershire, GL5 4EP

www.amberley-books.com

ISBN 978 1 4456 5225 2 (print)
ISBN 978 1 4456 5226 9 (ebook)

British Library Cataloguing in Publication Data.
A catalogue record for this book is available from the
British Library.

Typesetting by Amberley Publishing.
Printed in Great Britain.

Contents

Acknowledgements

I must acknowledge the help given to me by the staff of the Harris Community Library in Preston who willingly assist as I delve into their archives; their records of the period making my research that much easier.

My appreciation also goes to the newspaper reporters of the past who, in chronicling the events of the past two centuries, made this book possible. The *Preston Guardian, Preston Chronicle, Preston Pilot, Preston Herald* and, of course, the *Lancashire Evening Post* all provided information from their publications. The Preston historians of old, particularly Anthony Hewitson, Peter Whittle, Charles Hardwick, Henry Fishwick and William Pollard, provided me with valuable sources of information.

Besides my own collection of images/illustrations, I would like to thank the *Lancashire Evening Post* for permission to use images that are nowadays stored in the Preston Digital Archive. Also my thanks go to Richard H. Parker the creator of the PDA for use of images from that source and to Mike Hill, Communities Editor of the *Lancashire Evening Post*, who encourages my research into local history.

My thanks also to Pat Crook for cheerfully checking my text and putting her literary skills at my disposal once again.

Introduction

The research involved in compiling this book enabled me to understand some more about the city of Preston in Lancashire. I hope this manuscript will unlock many of the secrets of the past, be it from musty old manuscripts, fragile parchments, dusty old record books or yellowing newspapers from a bygone age.

The history of our nation tells us that amongst those who roamed these lands in far gone days were Romans, Saxons, Danes, Norwegians and Normans. They all laid claim to domination or ownership of our people and lands, often from far flung points.

It is unclear when the first settlements were built on the site of modern day Preston, but there have been several finds that indicate that as long ago as 10,000 BC some early inhabitants roamed here, and by 5,000 BC they were equipped with axe and spear. Those early settlers in Preston were few, and lived for the most part in tents or huts, and were always hunting when not fighting with hostile tribes. From Roman times we know of the fort at Ribchester and a staging post at Walton and of the Roman roads that passed through this region.

The record books show that as long ago as AD 705 lands on the Ribble, near Preston in Amounderness, were granted to Ripon Monastery and in AD 930 Athelstan, a Saxon King, saw fit to grant Preston to the Archbishop of York.

Such is the tangled web of early history that by 1080, when the Domesday Survey was begun, Preston was the chief town in Amounderness. The outline of Lancashire began to emerge when Roger of Poitou, a hero of the Battle of Hastings, was granted all lands between the Mersey and the Ribble, the county of Lancashire being established in 1182.

Significant events of the twelfth century saw monks from Normandy located at Tulketh Hall in 1124, privileges granted by Henry II in 1154, a charter granted by him in 1179 and a further charter granted by King John in 1199.

Records show Preston was clearly on the map in the thirteenth century. An assessment for tax made in 1218 recorded Preston as the wealthiest town in Lancashire, the Grey Friars arrived in 1221, Henry III granted a Charter in 1227 and another in 1252, and made a grant of land in the 'Forest of Fulwood' to the burgesses of Preston in 1253. The hospital of St Mary Magdalen was founded in 1293 and in 1295 the first recorded Parliamentary election was held at Preston.

In truth for almost 1,000 years Preston was simply a rural market town that developed around the church from where the original settlement grew. It became something of a significant crossroads with a handy river crossing. Preston suffered from famine, plague and warfare yet grew into a large industrial town, noted for its cotton and engineering industries and with all the trials that created as folk flocked to the important county town.

All these events helped to shape the Preston that grew into our city. Of course, much of the history of a city often lies beneath centuries of decay and development. Indeed, a dweller of the old town of Preston of centuries ago would simply be lost in our city streets these days.

Traditions that remain often enthral us and these socially motivated events bind the generations together. What our ancestors taught us is often treasured. Pageantry, parade, custom, folklore, festivals all leave a legacy of what they achieved. It is never just about the bricks and mortar, but the buildings help us to understand our ancestors' hopes and ambitions.

Hopefully, these chapters will bring to life some of the characters of old who walked along these highways and byways before us, leaving behind a trail that fascinates us and helps us to understand what kind of life they enjoyed, or endured.

Like all cities it is one of changing faces and changing places – indeed our Market Square is a prime example of that. Graveyards and bones, monks and monasteries, alleyways and tunnels, factories and workshops, plagues and poverty, pain and torment, disease and death, famine and feast all provide an insight into the past.

Curiosity led me to some of the discoveries and my admiration for the historians of old Preston does not waver, for they left a paper trail that can be clearly followed to unlock secrets of the past. It is often only necessary simply to scratch the surface to uncover parts of our past history, although our treasured archaeologists have dug much deeper for the cause.

My conclusion on delving, once more, into the history of Preston is that it is a place always full of pride, passion and people who cared about the place they called home.

Journey back with me into the secret past of Preston and loiter a while, and maybe marvel at those who lingered in olden days on the streets and fields of Preston past and their achievements.

The dictionary definition of secret includes the terms – concealed, unseen, and mysterious – not deliberately, of course, but as a result of the passage of time – hopefully some of the dust of time is blown away in the pages that follow.

A busy Preston Market Square c. 1844, with timber-framed properties built around 1630 on the south side of the Market Place, behind the original Moot/town hall. The land was earmarked for the erection of the new Gothic style town hall opened in 1867.

The Shambles where butchers plied their trade in nineteenth-century Preston.

A Market Square Steeped In History

Like many a town or city the Market Square in Preston is regarded as the centre of activity, and so it has proved to be down the centuries. Viewing it today it hides many secrets of Preston past. There is little doubt that Preston's Market Place is forever changing. The last significant change occurring in 2004 when the renovated Crystal House, that much maligned structure which stands where a succession of town halls once stood, was unveiled as the Cubic.

In the old Moot Hall days mayors and bailiffs would meet on the Market Place and discuss the town's affairs. Here in the open square at the ancient cross, friars discoursed and the devout prayed; here the inhabitants would meet for their amusement, in the form of bear and bull baiting; here delinquents were punished by means of the pillory; here for centuries the Guild Merchant has been proclaimed, and here until early in the nineteenth century most of the town's marketing took place.

Back in August 1617, at the foot of the Market Cross the town clerk greeted James I, who was on his way to Hoghton Tower and, of course, many a fight was waged in the Market Place between Royalist and Parliamentarian during the parliamentary unrest. At the Restoration, Charles II was proclaimed here amid great rejoicing, and subsequently the monarch granted the borough a charter. The Old Pretender was proclaimed at the Market Cross in 1715, and thirty years later the Young Pretender was greeted equally enthusiastically. The next day he marched triumphantly out of town and not many days later, on his retreat, he marched through town again with a dwindled and bedraggled following.

In the early part of the eighteenth century an obelisk was erected on the site of the old Market Cross, but this fell down and the Corporation replaced it in Guild Year 1782 with a more impressive one, which in 1816 had a gas lamp fitted on top. This obelisk was taken down in 1853 and portions of it were used in the gateway and walls of Hollowforth House in Woodplumpton. Amazingly, in 1979 this obelisk was returned to its rightful home in the Market Place where it once more proudly stands.

Towards the end of the nineteenth century great changes were afoot. In October 1893 the Harris Free Library and Museum were opened by the Earl of Derby after over a decade of planning and building. To make way for the museum a number of business premises on the east side of the Market Place had been demolished including a boot and shoe warehouse, a tea and coffee merchant's, a poultry and game dealer and the ironmonger's premises belonging to Joseph Bithnell Hallmark who was twice Mayor of the Borough. Another victim of progress was the area known as the 'New Shambles' where butchers had done business for decades.

Just as the museum was opening, work was beginning on the north side of the Market Place to demolish the old premises there and those that led down the doomed New Street, a narrow dark passageway, the changes making Friargate more accessible into the bargain. The reason for this was the intention to build the Central Post Office that opened for business in October 1903 serving the community for almost a century. Alongside this building scheme, at the corner of the Market Place a new place of justice was commenced with the construction of the Preston Sessions House.

Many people visited the Market Place in October 1904 to witness the unveiling of a granite obelisk in memory of the gallant soldiers of the Loyal North Lancashire who had fallen during the recent war in South Africa. This impressive ceremony to honour seven officers and 117 soldiers was led by a parade of civic and military dignitaries.

Should you wish to visit this monument these days then a visit to Avenham Park is required, because in 1925 it was removed to make way for the Cenotaph, built to remind us of the even greater losses during the First World War.

Along the western aspect of the Market Square, addressed as Cheapside, the properties have continually changed down the years, bearing little resemblance to those of a century ago, except for the small gable-ended shop premises that carry the name of Thomas Yates, a nineteenth-century local watchmaker who earned a silver medal for his design of a Dead-Beat Lever watch.

As the twentieth century dawned Preston was more than happy about its southern aspect with its Gothic-style town hall a source of great pride. This building had been opened in October 1867 with its magnificent clock tower and its Westminster chimes that

The Boer War Memorial unveiled in October 1904.

An engraving of the Market Place *c.* 1868 with the new town hall standing proud.

struck every quarter of an hour. The town hall replaced one completed in Guild Year 1782 that was a plain brick building with stone facings and with shops on the basement level, this particular town hall having succeeded one that had partially collapsed in June 1780.

However, by 1860 those in power thought that this gloomy looking brick structure that fronted on to Fishergate and had shops and houses dating back to 1619 to its rear, facing the Market Square, was no longer suitable for a growing town. After much debate it was agreed to demolish the entire block and build the large and stately edifice that Preston grew to love.

Politicians have given rousing speeches from the Harris Museum and the old town hall steps; footballers of Preston North End have held trophies aloft and prominent folk have been acclaimed by large crowds gathered in the Market Square.

It seems, though, that change is inevitable and on a dark night in March 1947 the much cherished town hall was engulfed by flames and left a fire-ravaged ruin. It took some fifteen years before the building was eventually demolished and for a time the square became a rectangle. Eventually from the rubble emerged Crystal House, a structure to which some took instant dislike, referring to it as an eyesore on the Market Square landscape. The newly cladded structure with prime retailers around its ground floor perimeter now has a twenty-first century look about it and is known as the Cubic.

In The Name of Harris – Quite A Transformation

Following the reading of the will of Edmund Robert Harris and his gift of £122,000 for the building of the Harris Free Library, Art Gallery & Museum the east side of the Market Square underwent a remarkable transformation, as these two images show.

The view of the east side of the Market Square *c.* 1875. The Preston Corporation provided the site at a cost of £30,000, and a number of old established business were removed.

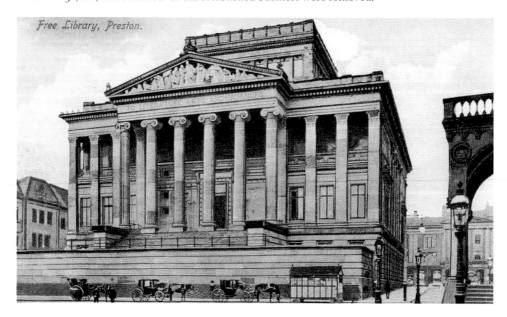

This early twentieth-century postcard shows the transformation on that side of the Market Square.

Around The Town with Richard Aughton

Richard Aughton was the son of a local builder and was clerk of works on a number of building projects in the Preston of the nineteenth century. In 1892 he took it upon himself to record his recollections of Preston in the period from 1830 to 1850. This feature uses those recollections to take a tour along our city streets today, giving us the opportunity to see what a difference there is from those far gone days described in the words of Richard Aughton.

The Parish Church (now St John's Minster), when I was a youth, had a quick thorn hedge some five feet high, growing from Church Street to the top of Stoneygate, and up to what was called the bone house and later the hearse house. At the back, and along the east side were brick walls. The graveyard could be entered by a flight of stone steps. The Church Street side eventually had a stone wall erected with stone steps into the front graveyard. The improvements cost much time and expense. I remember the removal of many corpses, and a great outcry was raised.

Rear view of the parish church recalled by Richard Aughton.

The church had formerly a massive tower, access to the top of which was obtained by narrow stone steps from the back. Many times did I along with young companions view processions from its summit. The top was covered with lead, and the roof of the church also. All the pews had perpendicular backs, the floors were covered with straw matting. The wardens and the Corporation sat in the front seats. The Revd Carus Wilson was the Vicar, he was a tall and very kind man. He lived in Winckley Square and under his able management were built St Mary's, St Thomas's, Christ Church and St James's.

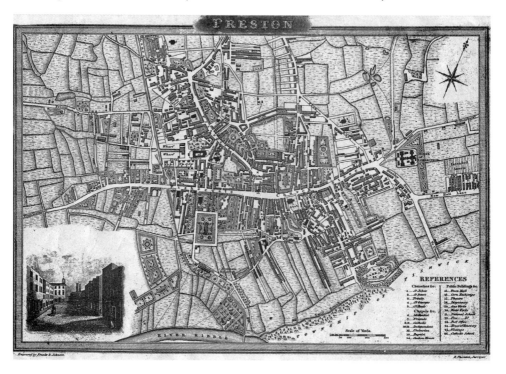

Above: A map of Preston in 1824, by Edward Baines.

Left: Revd Carus Wilson could be forgetful at times.

I remember the Vicar borrowing and forgetting to return so many umbrellas from Mr Latham, the architect in the office I worked in on Cross Street, that he determined to paint inside one of them the following inscription 'Stolen from John Latham, architect, Cross Street'. Well, the very next morning the Vicar called to borrow an umbrella, as there was a very heavy downpour of rain. Unfortunately, as the only person in the office I handed him the article. The Vicar walked off up Glover Street with it, but soon returned, saying, 'If you play me any more pranks I shall not be pleased; but give my compliments to Mr. Latham.'

Stoneygate, some fifty years ago, on the right hand side of the church from the corner of the graveyard to the angle opposite the White Lion Inn, consisted of fruit gardens, and extended back to a ditch eight yards wide, called Bull Dyke. It took all the refuse and the drainage from the Bull Hotel and stables. This ditch continued into another which came from Shepherd Street and went along towards Avenham Street and out again near Cannon Street Chapel, behind Cross Street Museum. It came out again at the bottom of Butler Street, under the railway, and behind the houses on Fishergate Hill.

The lower end of what is now called Walton's Parade, the land up to the end of West Cliff and on the slope to Fishergate Hill was used for market gardening, and the land now occupied by the West Lancashire Railway Station, extending to the Penwortham highway, was utilised for strawberry gardens. A tunnel was formed at the lower end of Charles Street for a road to the cliff, where stands the large brick house, then occupied by the Revd Clay the prison chaplain. The tunnel was only some four yards wide, and in dry weather was much used by pedestrians. At the north-east end there was a good spring of water, which was much used by gardeners. The tunnel is, I believe, now under a portion of the North Western Railway Station platforms.

In Charles Street was Robert Lowe's the banker's house. His bank was opposite the Parish Church, and he moved to opposite the Lancaster Bank. During a gale of wind, a chimney stack was blown down, and one of his daughters was killed. He at once left the house and beautiful gardens that extended nearly the whole length of Charles Street.

Down the sides and at the top of Charles Street grew large lime trees. Partly at the east corner of Charles Street into Fishergate a very large house stood, occupied by William Marshall. He was an active director of the railway. The house being built on the very edge of the railway tunnel under Fishergate. This tunnel was pulled up to make way for the present wide iron girder bridge. The London & North Western and Lancashire & Yorkshire Railway Companies Station was a large wooden shed on timber posts, some 12 inches square, all whitewashed. The present handsome island station and offices were constructed under Mr Axon the resident engineer.

In those days many of the chapels and churches were lighted by candle, as also were the workshops. The scholars at the schools were even ordered to provide candles.

The tramway skirted the back of Chapel Street, passed over a wooden bridge at the bottom of Garden Street, and along the back walls of the gardens to Ribblesdale Place, thence to the summit of Avenham Park to near the present flagstaff. Here the horses were detached from the wagons, which were hooked on to a very strong endless chain. This chain passed over a grooved wheel on an upright shaft, which revolved by steam engine power in the building adjoining.

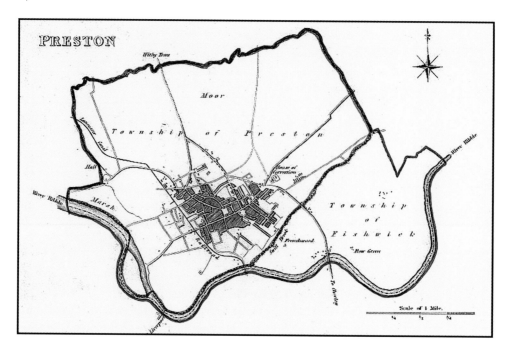

Map of 1835 – Showing Townships of Preston & Fishwick.

Avenham Park consisted to a great extent of garden ground, let off in small plots. In the gardens was a rustic cottage, in which resided a Mr Jackson.

The park now called Miller Park was used for growing vegetables and strawberries. When the London & North Western Railway Company was laying the bridge pier foundations such large masses of ice came down the river that fears were entertained for the safety of the coffer dams, and cannon were brought to discharge balls against the ice. The river often laid the ground occupied by the present Parks deep under water, destroying the fruit.

From Garden Street we get into Ribblesdale Place, all the land on the north side was a field right up to Avenham House. Cross Street was very rough and unpaved. To get to Camden Place there was only a footpath. The whole of the sites occupied by the houses on the east side of Camden Place and on the north side of Ribblesdale Place, up to and including the Mechanics Institute consisted of field or gardens. The Mechanics Institute was removed from Cannon Street, then that building was used for the waterworks and the *Preston Guardian* printing offices. Avenham Walks were entered through two iron gates. The walks extended to the south end of Bushell Place, and terminated with a stone wall. Glover Street was all a field. Near the bottom, on the opposite side from Cross Street, was a steep way leading to Avenham Street where there was a constant running of water which was free to all. Scores of people I have seen waiting to fill their buckets. Behind in the yard was a circular reservoir some 50 feet in diameter. The gas offices are partly built on its site. I forgot to mention a spring of water on the road side at the end of Avenham Colonnade, which supplied many of the tenants at Avenham. There was also a good stone trough for water to supply the tramway horses opposite, now, the steps leading to the lower side of Avenham Park.

Jackson's cottage on the Avenham Valley.

From Winckley Square; southwards fields and pasture aplenty.

Avenham House had plenty of pasture land around it.

Leaving the end of Avenham Street, opposite the John O'Gaunt public house, on the north side all the houses had low and thatched roofs, and about opposite to Gorst Street was a four storey building. At an earlier date there was a workhouse. Thence forward to the National School. Nearby were low thatched houses the floor being three feet below Avenham Lane pavement. All the ground opposite from Oxford Street to Albert Street consisted of green fields called Walker's. Walker had his horses pasturing there and his foundry at the bottom of Avenham Street. At the top of Albert Street, where St Augustine's Church now stands, and at the top of Oxford Street thousands upon thousands of bricks were made by hand labour for Ralph Dickson, who was also a timber dealer in North Road. From the south end of Duke Street, down a narrow steep footpath, access could be had to a good spring of water.

Along the footpath known as Swillbrook at an early morn could be met keen rod fishing gentlemen, such as John Gillet, Cuddy Holland and William McClellan, a grocer, who had his shop in the corner of the Market Place, adjoining the Cross Keys public house. These and many others have returned with good baskets of salmon caught near Walton Bridge, or Brockholes Half Penny Bridge, or down near to the Tram Railway Bridge. Many a nice salmon or more has Mr McClellan given me for my father.

Coming up what is now called London Road, on the south west side, all the ground was occupied by gardens till you came opposite the Rosebud Inn. There were the cotton mills

Plenty of keen fishermen would take the Swillbrook path down to the River Ribble to catch salmon. Engraving *c.* 1880.

of John Paley, and partly at the back Horrockses, Miller & Co. Yard Works, very extensive then, but now much larger.

Old Mr Horrocks lived at Lark Hill, now the Catholic School. He was a very stout, red faced, quiet gentleman. Queen Street was noted for all the tenants to be hand loom weavers. The space between the Blue Bell Inn and Grimshaw Street was occupied by the Earl of Derby's stables, fine and strong built structures. On the west side of Grimshaw Street lived John Robinson, timber merchant. He was so very stout and troubled with gout that it was said he had a plank laid down the stairs so that he could be slid into his brougham carriage. There were also two brothers named Hamer. John Hamer lived last in Ribblesdale Place. They were very liberal in their contributions to all religious objects.

The Independent Chapel was a square brick building, with two porticos at the front entrance. The school, under the back gallery, was lighted by candles; the choir had both string and wind instruments, and sat under the pulpit. The Revd Richard Slate was the minister – a little gentleman – who lived in Great Avenham Street. The chapel was built some six yards further back from the street. The land was used as a burial ground.

Beginning again at the bottom of Grimshaw Street we pass up Church Street and come to the Dog Inn, which was noted for the immense number of carts etc. which stopped there early in the morning laden with people going from East Lancashire to Lea Marsh or Lytham to bathe. They, being joined by all manner of conveyances from Preston, made up a long procession – no railway then.

Some 20 yards nearer the Parish Church from the Dog Inn was the post office. Two ladies were the post-mistresses, and Mr Johnson was the first letter deliverer. He wore very large spectacles. His son – one of the wittiest of men – assisted him, but he did not mind keeping people waiting for their correspondence if he could only have half an hour's chat with servant maids. When letters were asked for, the inquirer stood at the window in the lobby. The postage of a letter, say to Liverpool, was 8d. All the mails were carried by coach with four horses; the driver and guard wore red coats, and all passenger and mail coaches for Blackburn, Wigan, Liverpool, Manchester and Lancaster, departed from or arrived at the Red Lion, Bull Hotel, Crown or Legs of Man. The fare to Blackburn was 2s 6d, and to Liverpool 5s 6d. Besides this, the drivers expected a fee and woe be to the passenger on his next journey if he had forgotten this.

The winters sixty years ago were different from what we experience now. The writer has gone to school through cut snow two feet deep, and for miles on the route of the mail coaches have the public cut the way. We now turn by the east end of the parish church, and by the back of it we see the Cockpit. The houses on the side abutting Stoneygate were thatched, and had gardens. The Cockpit was used very shortly before 1830 for cock mains. It was afterwards used as a Temperance lecture hall. The first teetotal pledge was signed there. The writer remembers pushing his way inside. Here it was he saw the late Joseph Livesey experimenting and showing the nature of alcohol. On one occasion the writer was to carry the dishes containing beer and spirits. However, he and other youths put water into them. When the dish of water was on the table Mr. Livesey got a lighted candle and told the large audience they would see the blue flame of alcohol burn. But no flames arising, he applied his nose, and then exclaimed, 'Ah, my young friends have played on us a joke.' The writer was never asked to assist in the experiment again. The hall was often used for discussions on Mormonism, then very rife, and also on politics.

Mr Livesey was a cheese factor, and first sold cheese, in very small quantities, standing at Syke Hill, from a three-legged table. He was a most genial, kind hearted, and liberal man.

In Shepherd Street was the Grammar School, a long narrow building. The lower room was a day school. Mr Sedgwick was the master. At the east end was Dr Shepherd's Library, free to all who obtained an annual ticket from the mayor. The public entrance was from steps in the yard behind what is now the Arkwright Arms beer house, but there was a door for the schoolmaster's entrance from the school.

The large house, recently the Arkwright Arms beer house, was a beautiful residence, with a garden and large trees planted front and back. The headmaster of the Grammar School, the Revd Robert Harris, with his two sons and daughter, lived in it. Arkwright previously here invented the spinning jenny. There was an assistant-master, the Revd William Harrison, who lived in the top house in Stoneygate, near the Hearse House. Mr Harrison was very partial to Lundyfoot snuff. If a scholar was not fully prepared with his home lessons, half an ounce of snuff would see all right. There was also a Mr Peppercorn, the writing master, who was also partial to snuff. He lived in Grimshaw Street.

In those days, holidays were sometimes demanded, and if refused, one boy would arise from his seat and take his cap, the remainder of the scholars following him out. The first day of November, when the mayor was elected, was earnestly looked forward to; teachers and scholars, probably to the number of 100, used to assemble in the council chamber of the town hall to partake of the mayor's hospitality in the shape of fruit, cakes and wine.

There were very few cabs then, and sedan chairs were often used. The sedan chair was a kind of square box, with glass sides and doors. It was carried by two long poles pushed

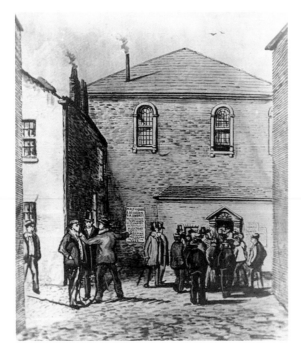

The Cock Pit building on Stoneygate became a meeting place.

through staples, and held hand high by two men. At night each had a horn lantern with a candle in. The carriers lived in St John's Street. They were always required for carrying old ladies and gentlemen to parties, where they were deposited in the lobby. They were also often used for children's funerals, the female adults being inside with the coffin, the ends of which protruded through the glass of the doors.

There was a warehouse in Stoneygate, opposite the Hearse House, used by Mr Goodair as a place for taking in the cloth woven by hand. He removed to the Malt Kilns at Larkhill, formerly worked by a Mr Dean. Mr Goodair erected the large cotton mills and worked them with an old mill adjoining. He was a very clever and shrewd man.

At the corner of St John's Place, in line with the back wall of the church, lived a very notorious man of the name of James Duckworth, but always called 'Touch' Duckworth. He kept two or three racehorses and very old trotting horses and gigs for hire, but allowed no one to use a whip. He also kept fighting dogs and bull dogs, game fowls and pigeons, and a large black bear. All were lodged in the cellar. One morning three bailiffs called for rent. He happened to be out at the time, but when he returned his wife told him who was in the parlour. He went to them and said, 'I have no money, but if you will wait ten minutes you shall have something.' He at once fetched the bear, seeing which the bailiffs got through the windows as quickly as possible and vanished.

At Syke Hill there was a public pump, with wood stoops in a large circle around it. At that time nearby all the streets and footpaths were composed of round boulders, brought in boats to the Old Quay from Lytham. In Paradise Street and Vauxhall Road were public bake houses, for not much cooking was attended to at home. There was one also at the bottom of Pleasant Street. To these places bread and dinners were taken from the neighbourhoods, and what we now call yeast was barm. I remember seeing scores of children waiting in line for a halfpennyworth at six in the morning at a beer house at the corner of William Street.

The Bull Hotel, kept by Mrs Scott, was considered the Tory house. The writer has seen every window broken by the Liberal party, once notably, when navvies were specially brought from Fleetwood, and as Sir Hesketh Fleetwood had just commenced to build that town, and was offering himself as a candidate for MP, they came with truncheons, and wore specially made blue caps. They pulled up the street pavement for missiles. In two or three nights afterwards the opposite party did similar damage to the Red Lion Hotel. £3, £4 and £5 were given for a vote, and the agents of the candidates would, if possible, get hold of voters and drive them to another town rather than have the vote given against them.

Most of the houses from the Bull Hotel to Avenham Street were thatched, and all the shops to Cannon Street were small and low. The shop at the corner of Cannon Street, now occupied by a fruiterer, was occupied by Mr Edward Waterworth, a grocer. In his shop generally during a morning, might be seen himself, Peter Haydock, Richard Threlfall, Roger Tuson, Richard Aughton, and some two or three more discussing the town's news, or scheming some plan to develop the Ribble navigation. At eight o'clock at night, for two hours, many of them assembled in their private room at the Red Lion to talk over the same subject. They were named the 'doves' and woe to him who in any manner disturbed them.

At the two corners of Cannon Street stood two large iron cannons, fixed with breaches in the ground. Near the top of Mount Street a very celebrated old woman, named Betty

Redhead, lived. She would walk up and down Fishergate with any lady or gentleman passing at the time, and leave her sweet-meat shop all open. She generally had on only a large mob cap and red shoulder shawl. From the theatre to Butler Street, as also on the opposite side to Charnley Street, only wooden railings with fields or gardens, were visible. From Charnley Street to Lune Street were good houses, and the dispensary, around the front doors and windows of which grew vines, and many bunches of grapes has Mr Walker, the stationer, given me.

Lune Street is something like it was in 1830, except that the site of the cabinet and furniture warehouses was vacant land and what were private houses are now shops, the Savings Bank, and Hardings Livery Stables. The Wesleyan Chapel was a very plain brick fronted building set back from the street 15 yards, with plain iron palisades in line of the street.

The public hall was called the Corn Exchange. It was an open area into which the farmers with grain could bring their laden carts. At the time there were four wind corn mills in the borough. The front enclosed space in the front centre of the Corn Exchange was occupied by cheese factors; the sides on the ground, and the front outside pavement, were for the sale of butter. At that time housekeepers attended in scores, trying the samples and purchasing. At the west end, or back, was the pork market. At each side and one end there were iron pillars to support a room open to the area used by woollen cloth merchants, as also a room higher; but during the fairs they were devoted to toy stalls.

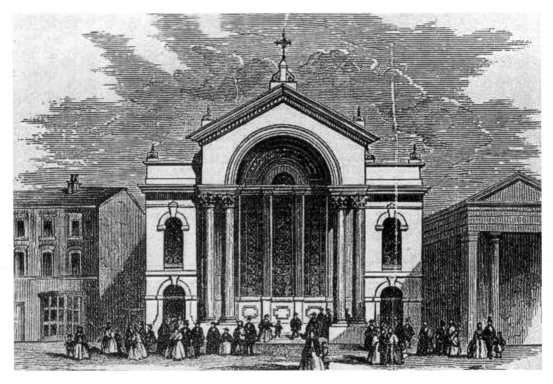

A familiar sight on Lune Street was the Wesleyan Chapel built in 1817 – nowadays the Central Methodist Church.

A little below the Mitre Inn, in Fishergate, was a public pump. Partly at the corner into the Market Place was Mr Watson's saddler's shop. Thomas Prescot, who worked from him, succeeded to it. He was a very little man, but one of the drollest. His shop was like a news shop. Nearly every tradesman called upon him for the latest news.

The town hall in 1830 was very different in appearance to what it is now. The hall proper was entered by a flight of stone steps near the south east angle. These led to the space allotted for the public to hear the trials. The magistrate's bench was at the further windows overlooking the Straight Shambles. The Council Chamber looked into Church Street, and down Fishergate. In this room were held banquets, and on the first Sunday of the month the councillors and other gentlemen had hot spiced wine supplied. Over the entrance, in the tower, was the clock and a fine bell. On each side of the entrance door was fixed the javelins. The space under the town hall was occupied by hosiers' and hatters' and drapers' shops.

In the Market Place were very old wood framed shops and the public street weighing machines. The writer has seen the Market Place filled with straw and hay carts. At the Friargate end the Market Place had the fish stones; which consisted of six stone tables or counters fixed in a semi-circle. The vendors stood inside the circle. During fair time the pavement was covered with pots, and the public selected their articles from the ground. In the centre stood the obelisk, a very tall round pillar on five circular steps. In 1830 there was a bellman, dressed in Corporation livery. His duty was to announce fairs from the obelisk steps, and make various public announcements. At the conclusion he rang his bell, touched his hat, and said 'God Save the King'.

Leaving the town hall front and passing along Church Street, we would come across some celebrated houses which time fails me to fully describe. On the opposite side, and nearly in front of the town hall, is Main Sprit Wiend. Down this narrow lane was the Blue Coat School. The building was small. It was a free school. The master was a Mr Banks, whose salary was from endowments. I believe there is a board fixed on the wall stating who left the legacies. On the opposite side of the street was a tannery with six pits.

Where the Red Lion Hotel is now, the Government Excise officers met and received the taxes. The writer remembers going once with some £70 in gold to pay the duty on the probable number of bricks his father would make during the following three months, for which time every night a man counted what was made during the day, and not a brick might be made more than what duty had been paid. This one visit to pay the duty proved of serious consequences, for one of the sovereigns was bad so the officers said, at once it was clipped in two, so that I could not pay or find another. Next morning the brick field was closed until my father returned from the Manchester head office to pay the duty. He had to travel by coach.

Adjoining was the building of the Old Bank, the proprietors of which were Pedder, the father of the late Edward Pedder, and Fleetwood. The entrance had a portico on stone pillars. The front windows were narrow and short. Lower down was a private dwelling, afterwards the water offices, and Hudson and Lowe had their bank adjoining before they removed into Fishergate. Further down Church Street we come to the late Joseph Livesey's cheese warehouses. The upper rooms were used for printing his early papers, such as *The Struggle*, and his many temperance tracts and advocates.

Church Street, from Water Street to the town hall, on each side of the kerb stone, on a Saturday was occupied with butchers' stalls, and during the first whole week of January with the horse fair, and I have seen both sides of Fishergate, from the town hall to Lune Street, used for the sale of berries and fruit. I must not forget to mention that in 1830 night watchmen from 10 p.m. to 5 a.m. called aloud, as they walked the streets with a large hand swinging horn lantern, the state of the weather and the hour.

Opposite the bottom of Grimshaw Street was a very large house, occasionally occupied by the Earl of Derby. It was approached by a double flight of stone steps, which stood out partly on the present footpath. There were large iron gates at the bottom of a gravel walk to the house, and beautiful gardens some 8 feet above Church Street. There were also large gardens at the back. When the house was pulled down Earl Street was formed.

Above: A mansion fit for an earl on Church Street – knocked down in 1835.

Left: Revd J. Rigg would give up his breakfast to the poor.

In Church Street, nearly opposite the Horse Shoe public house, was a public pump, and a house that was built under a wager in one day. We now come to Park Road, and a large timber yard occupied by Mr Robinson and afterwards by Mr Aughton. The gaol or prison was very small compared to what it is now. A Miss Robinson was the governor and the Revd Mr Clay was the chaplain. Miss Robinson married Mr John Knowles, who had his corn warehouse in Lord Street, and lived in Lune Street. He was also a partner with his brother George at Cadley Wind Mill.

Up Ribbleton Lane, past the cottages on the right side and also on the left to Deepdale Road, was pasture land, and a large portion was cultivated with rhubarb by a Mr Grimshaw. During the season he loaded six or more carts with rhubarb, and sent them by road to Liverpool, these carts and others bringing back from Bank Bridge, in Tarleton, timber or cotton. On the opposite side of what is now St Mary's Street to an old rough lane called Acre Gate, was all brickfield, which extended to New Hall or Blackburn Road.

Back towards the town, in front of the cotton mills now near St Mary's Street, were three streets say 40 yards wide. On the two sides and up the middle were small cottages, with hand loom weaving places. They were only 9 feet high. On the opposite side of the road to the Rosebud Inn and down London Road was vacant land.

Beginning again in Ribbleton Lane, at the County Arms, the space on to the barracks was pasture fields. Coming from the Barracks, and near the Longridge Railway Bridge, was a long, large whitewashed building – the workhouse – and near it the present infirmary, then called the House of Recovery. It was surrounded by a strong, quick, thorn hedge. There was a miry lane passing on the west side to the brick fields, and a foot path that led to Moor Park. Meadow Street, and all the land on both sides up to St Ignatius Square, consisted of fields. From Meadow Street, opposite Stone Cottage – the first built off Meadow Street – was a footpath past Frank Sledden's and Birley's mills, which led over Lambert Bottoms to the Moor, now the Park. This passed the house garden wall of Moor Hall, occupied by Mr Walker, the solicitor, his three brothers and sister. Now it is a good street or road to about the centre of the avenue. The Park was used by Mr Matthew Brown, who was a great farmer.

Near Meadow Street is Pump Street. Here was a good well of water and a pump in a shed, which supplied large casks in a cart. The water was hawked in the streets of Preston at half a penny the six-gallon can. St Paul's Church, I well remember, had a very big clergyman, Mr Rigg, who was noted for his liberality. He would give his breakfast to a poor beggar. I remember seeing him once in Church Street without a coat. He was in his shirt sleeves, having just given his coat to a poor man. From the west end of Meadow Street we join Lancaster Road, and going north we come into the north mail coach road. This was all fields on both sides, except a cotton mill, owned by George Smith.

The church of the English Martyrs is erected on what was called Gallows Hill. The ground was formerly some ten yards higher. History tells us a battle was fought there, and the rebels hung. On Lancaster or Garstang Road, as denoted 1.5 miles from Preston, stood a toll bar, at the junction of Watling Street Road. All Fulwood Park was in fields, sold in allotments. The writer was about the third tenant.

The Turks Head lock up was recalled by Richard Aughton.

Returning to Preston on North Road, we cross over, in Lancaster Road, the Longridge Railway, but in 1830 there was no railway. All the stone was brought in carts, and then rails were laid from behind Barton Terrace for waggons, which were drawn by horses up to Longridge. They, with full waggons of stones, returned in or on an empty one. Then the railway for locomotives was continued chiefly in tunnels to Maudland. Lime was chiefly burnt at Chipping by a Mr Henry Wilkinson, and sent to Preston in carts. If we continue on towards Preston, we come down Walker Street to near the junction with the North Road having hedges on both sides.

Coming on to Preston by the North Road, we pass St Paul's Church and on to Church Street near the prison. There was a wind corn mill near the Wesley Chapel and also one called Kirkham's. It was about 200 yards more north than the other one. If we keep to the right we come into St John's Street. The length on the left hand to Lord Street consisted of barns, stables and cart sheds; on the opposite side were thatched roof cottages. Opposite the end of Lord Street was the Pig Market. At the corner was a tallow candle works run by Shakeshaft.

On the right of what is now called Ormskirk Road was the waterworks, then a warehouse. In the Orchard, where Lancaster Road comes in, there was a clay pipe making manufacturer. The writer remembers the Orchard when it was all spare land, and he thinks the Primitive Methodists were the first to build upon it. The Earl of Derby opened the street to Church Street.

The borough prison was first in Turk's Head Yard, then in Avenham Street. Mr Bannister was the Superintendent. The fire engines were also stationed here. The new Lancaster Road was then occupied by resident butchers. There was also a narrow street running off it, past the Shakespeare Inn, into the Market Place, used for sale of butchers' meat.

The Orchard of 1855 before the Covered Market was erected.

The Shambles as then called, were entered from Church Street, about the present position, but through a 7-foot passage. Making the way interfered with the Red Cross Inn and Stanley Arms. The Earl pulled this down, and rebuilt them where they now stand. He also had four other public houses pulled down which stood in a narrow crooked street, where now the north front of the present Public Library and Museum stands.

Commencing again at Garstang high road and coming to town, all land on the west side, and a large plot of the east of it, was pasture land. On the west near what is now the Adelphi Inn, was probably 15 yards high. It was sold for its valuable sand. On the east near, near the back of St Thomas's church, Mr Humber had a five sail windmill. Coming on we join Friargate. Here was a public pump, nearly opposite Walker Street. In Friargate we pass the Roast Beef public house. The street above her was lowered. See the front rooms of the Roast Beef Inn and the shops on the opposite side. The houses had to have stone steps on to the footpath. Among the old inhabitants of the old Market Place were Wilcocks & Dobson, tea dealers and the proprietors of the Preston Chronicle. Henry Walton, the auctioneer, had a woollen draper's shop and many other old shopkeepers I remember too numerous to mention.

Returning down Friargate, at the top of the hill we come to Bridge Street. At the bottom is a mill, which was for worsted; hence Canal Bridge is called the Worsted Bridge, and many times the writer has watched Lancaster passenger packet boat go or return. It was only about 7 feet wide, but 50 feet long, and was drawn by two horses with jockeys at about 8 miles an hour. When passengers were once in, they were not allowed to move about.

Lower down is the Saw Mill. When the chimney was nearly finished by some means the rope slipped over the top pulley, and the man at the top could not get down. After many and various methods had been suggested, and just as he was about to throw himself on to several beds laid on the ground, his wife shouted to him up the chimney to unravel

Preston was a town with plenty of windmills.

his new stockings. He did so, and to the first end dropped stronger twine was hoisted to him, till eventually he got the rope and came down to safety.

Near to the Saw Mill are several mills, which were worked by Furness & Co., for flax spinning. After Bow Lane all was green fields to the Marsh, which was used for pasture. At the bottom was a large outfall culvert, a large portion open.

At Bow Lane corner stood a pump. Commencing at the Adelphi Inn we joined Fylde Road. There was not any houses before we came to St Peter's church. Going under the then called Preston & Wyre Railway arches we come to the Marsh again. In the corner on the left was the Spa Cold Water Plunge Bath. It was most frequented throughout the year. The writer remembers meeting Thomas Prescott on a cold winter's morning. He said, 'I and three others are returning home from Spa. We had to break the inch thick ice and burn candles in horn lanterns to see the path,' and this was not an uncommon thing.

The way over the Marsh in continuation of Water Lane from Fylde Road led to warehouses, which were well used by such as Carrs, Horns and Humbers, corn merchants receiving grain from lighters or flats. Timber, also came up to the Victoria Quay, but a large quantity was discharged at Bank Bridge. Passing the warehouses was a road leading to a lane on to Ashton near the church. On the river front were several houses. Ashton from the church to now the railway was all arable land.

Now that I have jotted down something about men and places, a word or two about funerals might not be objectionable. There were very few mourning coaches. These were covered from the top edge half way down with black cloth, and the horses were black. There were only two hearses, quite plain, and they were not often used, except for the removal to a country churchyard. For the town funeral the coffin was laid on a bier, and

The Victoria Quay was becoming a busy place in days before the Docks.

borne on the shoulders of four, six or eight men to the grave, all the men and friends having had sent them kid gloves and silk hat bands. At the more respectable funerals the friends had shoulder bands of three yards of silk. All friends walked in pairs. The relatives wore bands of black crape, and it was expected that all would attend the place of worship on the following Sunday.

The undertakers received, as a rule, 2s 6d up to 5s, for attendance, in addition to their working wage, which then were 22s per week, beginning at six o'clock in the morning and finishing at six o'clock in the evening. All the undertakers wore black cloth clothes. The coffin in procession had a black cloth velvet pall thrown over, but for a young female it had a white silk fringe, 12 inches wide. All friends wore white gloves and bands tied with white ribbon. A William Eckersley, livery stable keeper, in Pitt Street, was the chief supplier of horses, and also William Harding, father of the present Hardings, in Lune Street and Fishergate. He opened his yard in Glover Street, adjoining the Wellington Inn.

Among well-known characters I must not forget to mention Jenny Aughton. She was a very little old woman, and for years had travelled with a horse and open cart the road from Southport to Preston twice weekly with cockles, shrimps, and fish. She arrived at six o'clock on a Saturday morning at the Grey Horse Inn, Fishergate. At one o'clock in the afternoon, when her parcels for Southport were collected she was off home. I suppose she travelled on this way for forty years. I rode with her several times, the journey taking about eight hours. Jenny Aughton was a great abstainer, I can only remember her being sick once for a week.

Richard Aughton's saunter through the streets of Preston of his early life had unlocked secrets from a time when the population of Preston grew from barely 34,000 to twice that number in 1850. Thanks therefore to a man who shared his secrets that many of those who wandered through the streets of Preston in 1892 had no recollection of, and of which we knew little.

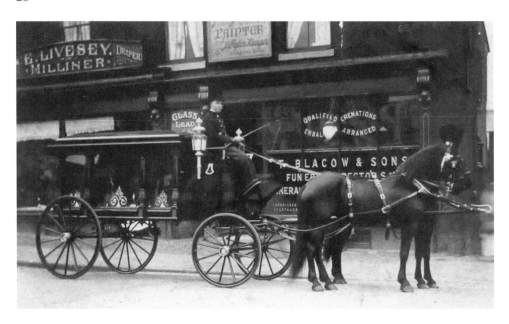

A funeral hearse and horses were a common sight in Preston

Punishment and Pastimes

The truth of life in olden times is that there were many peculiar pastimes and punishments including some that would today fill us with horror. On George Lang's map of 1774 one of the fields shown was marked as 'Cuckstool Pit Meadow.' The cucking or ducking stool was one of the public methods of punishment in Preston. The stool was a crudely made chair, fixed at the end of a long strong plank. The victim to be ducked, usually a gossipy housewife or servant, being fastened in the chair and the plank being pivoted over the water. The stool being moved up and down into the water, often with great fury.

This instrument of torture was commonplace on many a village green. Old churchwarden accounts show that in 1572 a carpenter was paid 8s for making such a stool and 10s for the timber and iron, while in 1625 a willing helper was paid 4 pence for his assistance at the cucking. Apparently this punishment did not always seem to be a deterrent because once unfastened the culprit often let flow a torrent of oaths and curses.

The pillory was also a means of punishment that folks of old had to endure. It consisted of two horizontal pieces of wood, fixed upon a post, and across the centre of the horizontals there were three round holes – the middle for the head, the others for the hands. The pillory was usually raised above ground level to ensure a good view of the wretched victim for public scrutiny. The Preston Court Leet records show that in

The cucking stool a punishment for a gossipy housewife.

1665 the provision of a pillory was requested. Originally, it was positioned at the east end of the town but later was set on the north side of the Market Place. Records show that in 1816 an elderly man was placed in that pillory after being convicted of keeping a disreputable house in Back Lane. Likewise, the stocks were often used, whereby the feet of an offender were also secured through cut openings, this often being a favourite place to punish the bad apprentice or drunken folk. Speaking at a lecture in 1849, historian Peter Whittle recalled the stocks in the Parish Church graveyard, remarking thus: 'In 1806 the stocks were close to a tombstone dated 1642 that was inscribed "In the memory of Richard Greenfield, who was slain in the lane near Walton Bridge, during the civil war." A rude outline was cut upon it of a man with a sword run through his body.'

To this day in the Preston Market Square near Cheapside you can still see evidence of the bull ring where the bulls were tied when being baited. The sport was declared illegal in 1835. It is on record that in 1656, the Corporation bought a bull, primarily for freeman's cattle and afterwards for baiting purposes. In Preston, although it eventually became adopted as an annual custom, it became a problem. It was cruel, yet an intensely national sport. Although the bull had only a circumscribed range, being tied by a rope to a ring fixed in the ground, the dogs did not always get the best of the combat, and many a dog met its death, or ended a limping cripple for the rest of its life. The Corporation declared in 1726 that it had caused very great disorder amongst the inhabitants, frequently causing rioting, affrays and bloodshed and in consequence, no bull would be bought or baited by them as it was regarded as dangerous to the public peace.

Cock fighting was another sport of great antiquity and schoolboys held cock fights on Shrove Tuesdays, and were encouraged by the elders. Indeed, cock fighting was a public enjoyment in Preston from very early times. In 1650 records show the town council complaining about the state of one in need of repair, and one existed in the basement of a building in Back Lane around 1780. On Lang's map, near to Adelphi Street there was a 'Cockpit Field.' The building last used in Preston for openly recognised cock fighting was at the lower end of St John's Place. Apparently the rabble were not admitted during the fighting, the results being shouted out of a window to the waiting crowd. In 1814 visitors to the parish church had cause to complain about the infernal yells and curses they could hear coming from that cockpit, which closed in 1830 or thereabouts.

Despite cock fighting being illegal from 1835, an underground movement still existed and in September 1862, during Preston Guild week, Edward Wilkinson and Richard Marginson appeared at the Preston Borough police court charged with arranging cock fighting. Two police constables testified to seeing the defendants carrying some cocks to a schoolroom adjoining the Sir Walter Scott public house on North Road. Later, on entering the room, the officers saw upwards of 150 persons assembled as two cocks fought. There were eleven cocks in all, but two had been killed. The schoolmaster was questioned and he stated that John Hobson, the landlord of the inn, had hired the room out in exchange for five shillings.

The two accused who admitted supplying the gamecocks, but denied arranging it, were duly fined twenty shillings each. Three weeks later Hobson, aged thirty-three, was in the dock charged with unlawfully staging the cock fighting. This time Marginson was called as a witness, and he testified that the publican had engaged him to provide the cocks, claiming all preparations for the event had been done by Hobson. Hobson remarked that cock fighting had taken place at the Guild of 1842 and he thought it would be permitted again. He claimed that he had not received any admission money, but had been asked to stage the event for employees of a local cotton mill as a Guild treat. The magistrates after a short discussion found the publican guilty and he was fined thirty shillings for staging the barbaric sporting contest.

The old Cock Pit building in Back Lane.

Foot races and horse races were likewise, in olden times, sources of popular pleasure. As long ago as 1675 a foot race over four miles was advertised at Preston during Easter week, with a purse of fifteen shillings for the winner. Horse racing was first run on the Preston Moor, in 1726 and was periodically continued until 1791. A stone still remains on Moor Park, reminding us of the finishing post of long ago.

Adding to the above were such events as trail dog hunting, with over fifty dogs scampering through the streets; colt-jumping, where participants had to leap over dams of water, and pump whipping, when newly elected bailiffs were broken in by being whipped round the town's pumps. The pump near the Waggon & Horses being the main place of the floggings, which eventually got out of hand and had to be banned. It is fairly obvious that these excessive pastimes and punishments belonged to a bygone age.

Those Uncivil War Days in Preston

During the civil wars of the seventeenth century, Preston was in turn held by the Royalists of Charles I and the Parliamentarians of Oliver Cromwell. Ardent supporters of Charles I from all over Lancashire and under the guidance of the Earl of Derby made plans for the recruitment of the King's forces. Subsequently, Preston was used as a garrison by soldiers on the Royalist side with upwards of 300 stationed there.

This action did not go unnoticed by Sir Thomas Fairfax, the Parliamentarian general, and early in February 1643 an army under the guidance of Sir John Seaton, a Parliamentarian high flyer, stormed Preston. Half his 3,600 troops were club men, regarded as savages who would slay anyone in their path. The army from the Manchester area attacked the town, which was fortified by an inner and outer wall to the south and the east.

The Parliamentary forces forced their way over the walls and drove the Royalists back into the town. One of the Royalist strongholds was the tower of the parish church where brave but futile resistance was attempted by a few Prestonians who fired muskets onto the rampaging throng. However, within a couple of hours the Parliamentarians had full control of the town. A number of leading Royalists were slain including Adam Morte and his son, as well as Captain Hoghton, the brother of Sir Gilbert Hoghton who at that time was the owner and occupier of Hoghton Tower. Adam Morte had been elected Mayor of Preston in 1642, but had declined the office and had been fined 100 marks for his contempt of the authorities. The weeks that followed were unsavoury in Preston's history with the victorious troops enjoying the spoils of war in the ale houses and taverns, scenes of debauchery and vice.

However, in March the Royalists seized an unexpected opportunity to regain control of the town. The county town of Lancaster was being sorely pressed by Royalist soldiers and General Seaton and Colonel Ashton left Preston with a number of the Parliamentarian forces, with the intention of relieving it. Quickly moving his soldiers from Lancaster, the Earl of Derby marched them to Preston, on an undetected route. Arriving in the town at 10 o'clock at night they called upon the garrison to surrender in the name of the king. Weakened through the withdrawals the Parliamentarians were compelled to surrender as Preston was plundered once more. Parliamentarians caught in the town were unmercifully slaughtered. Derby had hopes of retaking the whole of Lancashire for the king, but they were routed at Whalley and the survivors fled.

As the Royalist grip was lost in Lancashire the town once again changed hands, with the Earl of Derby's forces retreating in a northerly direction. Prince Rupert was not impressed with the authorities of Preston and during his retreat after the Royalist defeat at Marston Moor he visited the town. On account of their apathy to the Royalist cause he seized the Mayor, William Cottam, and the two bailiffs. They were imprisoned in Skipton Castle, where they remained for three months.

The first Civil War ended on the 5 May 1646 with the surrender of Charles I. His captivity was somewhat relaxed and he was able to secretly rally his cause and encourage national unrest. Parliament was distracted by its own political and religious squabbles and the Royalist forces began to re-emerge. In Scotland, the Royalist cause blossomed and in July 1648 the Duke of Hamilton headed south intent on restoring Charles I to the throne.

The Scots march south was slow, the bad weather, meagre provisions and lack of marching discipline hampered their progress. Before they reached Preston they were involved in a skirmish with the troops of Cromwell's lieutenant John Lambert. With Lambert blocking the way south through Yorkshire, the Hamilton forces headed towards Preston.

The Battle of Preston on the 17 August 1648 was a hard-fought one with the Scots unable to match the manoeuvring skills of Cromwell. The action began in the Ribbleton Moor area with Cromwell's New Model Army confronting the soldiers of Sir Marmaduke Langdale. The Roundheads faced fierce resistance and only when Ashton's Lancashire

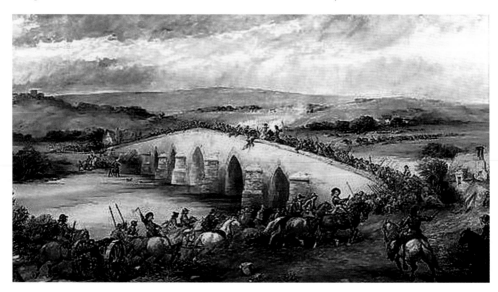

The battle for Walton Bridge was a bloody affair.

Horse and two other Regiments of Lancashire Foot joined the action did Langdale's forces retreat. The Roundheads had stormed into the fight, their pikes spearing Langdale's musketeers and broadswords slicing into groups of unsupported infantry.

As the fighting moved towards Preston a running battle began, as Hamilton's army and Cromwell's troops made for the bridge at Walton-le-Dale. The fighting was fierce, Hamilton led charge after charge at the stubborn Roundhead ranks. The Royalists were beaten off the bridge and chased over the nearby bridge crossing the River Darwen. The Scots troops gathered on the outskirts of Walton-le–Dale in a sorry state with morale shattered after the day's engagements. It is said that Oliver Cromwell and his army of 7,000 troops put up for the night in the village.

Behind them lay a devastated Preston, buildings battered, windows smashed and 1,000 Royalist corpses left wallowing in the mud. In front, just a musket shot away, the remnants of the Scottish Royalist Army who were making ready to sneak off in disarray. Any realistic Royalist hopes had been dashed. In truth, Preston folk looked forward to the end of constant military activity. Troops passing through town had for too long been plundering and causing mayhem on the streets.

Cromwell pursued the Royalists in the following days and gave them a severe drubbing at Winwick Church. Many of the survivors from Preston died of their wounds and sickness, whilst others drifted away into the countryside.

The Parliamentarians had had enough of the Royalists and unlike after the first Civil War, they showed no leniency this time. Hamilton was eventually captured and executed, and Charles I paid the price for the defeat of his Scottish allies when he was beheaded at Whitehall.

THE BATTLE OF PRESTON.

The Battle of Preston was hard fought.

Short Lived – The Peace of Preston

In the rebellion of 1715, provoked by the death of the last Stuart monarch, Queen Anne, and the accession of George I, the Roman Catholics of Lancashire were on the side of the Pretender James Edward Stuart, son of James II. Consequently amongst his supporters in Preston and its neighbourhood were many of the oldest, trusted and leading families. They had not forgotten the bitter persecution to which their ancestors had been subjected. The breaking out of the rebellion in Scotland was hailed with delight by the Jacobites in Manchester, who pledged to raise an army of 20,000 men.

The Scottish forces arrived in Lancaster on 7 November 1715 and James Francis Edward Stuart was proclaimed as king. Elated with their success, a couple of days later they set out for Preston. The Horse Regiment reached Preston on the night of the 9 November and they found that the two troops of Stanhope's Dragoons, formerly stationed there, had removed upon their approach. This gave them great encouragement, and caused them to imagine that the king's troops would not meet them in open combat.

The day was very sombre, rain pouring in torrents from the heavens, making the high roads very bad, in consequence they left the foot soldiers at Garstang with orders to advance the next morning, which was accomplished. On their arrival in the town, they marched up to the cross, in the Market Place, and were drawn up in regular order, while the Pretender was proclaimed – declaring that James VIII, son of the deceased James VII, be the lawful king, by the Grace of God.

The insurgents were joined by a great many gentlemen, together with their tenants, servants and others, who were chiefly of the Catholic faith. They resolved amongst themselves to march out of Preston and onwards on the Saturday.

During this time they were unaware that the king's troops were on the march towards Preston and busily preparing to give them battle. To their surprise they heard reports that General Charles Wills was advancing from the town of Wigan to attack them. Messengers from all parts confirmed the fact, giving cause for the peaceful inhabitants of Preston to be put in bodily fear.

Under General Forster's instructions, a body of men marched straight out of town to the Ribble Bridge and posted themselves there, Gen. Forster going further with a party of horsemen to gain accounts of the invasion force. The foot soldiers who advanced to the bridge were about 100, all choice, stout and well-armed men, commanded by Colonel Farquharson, part of Laird Mackintosh's battalion.

Farquharson was a superior officer and very intrepid man who would have defended the bridge until the last drop of blood; but he was ordered to retreat. This retreat appeared ill timed and later was highly condemned. The river was only fordable above and below the bridge which they might have made impassable; as for the bridge they might have barricaded it so well that it would have been impossible for the king's troops to have passed. They had cannon also, which Gen. Wills had not and the advancing army would have been exposed to their firing.

When General Wills was told that the rebels had abandoned their posts he was surprised, but felt they may be waiting in the hedgerows to confront them. The road was very deep, and so narrow in those days that two men struggled to ride abreast. When it was realised the highway was clear he thought that the rebels had fled, and gone from Preston. But he soon obtained news that they had retreated into the town and secured themselves there, awaiting an attack.

General Wills had nothing to do but prepare forthwith and, having advanced near the town, he ordered his troops to pass on the left hand gateways which led to some fields that lay behind the town, and by this means spread the enclosures with his men.

During this time the rebels were busily employed in the town, applying themselves resolutely by barricading the various streets bylanes, and houses. The gentlemen volunteers were drawn up in the churchyard under the command of James Radcliffe, Earl of Derwentwater, who encouraged his men by giving them money and fair words, and animated them to make a vigorous defence.

When Lord Derwentwater had prepared the defence, he ordered Mr Patten, the Jacobite chaplain, to bring him regular news from the various quarters of the town, relative to the attack and where men were required to maintain the siege. Mr Patten fully complied with the task and in the course of his perambulations he had his horse shot from under him.

The rebels formed four main barriers within the town; one a little below the church near Clarkes yard, commanded by Brigadier Mackintosh; the gentleman volunteers in the churchyard, were fixed there to support that barrier; Lord Charles Murray supported

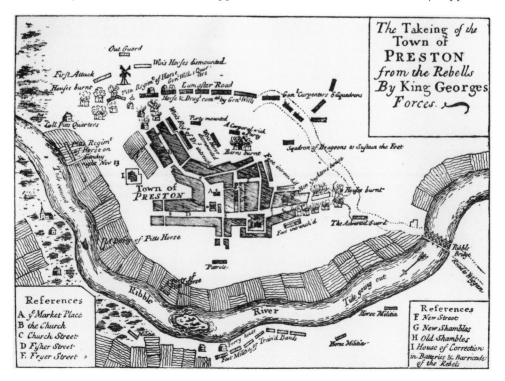

Preston – the battle ground of 1715 as the Rebels attempted to quell the King's forces.

the barrier which was fixed at the lane called Water Street (now Manchester Road); the third barrier was titled the Windmill barrier, and was commanded by Colonel Mackintosh; and the fourth was situated in the street leading towards Liverpool called Fishergate, and was commanded by Major Miller.

The three former posts were attacked with great violence by His Majesty's troops. The first attack was made on that barrier below the church, commanded by Brigadier Mackintosh. They met with such a resistance and incessant firing was made upon them from the barricade and the houses on either side, that Gen. Willis ordered the party to retreat to the entrance of the town. During the heat of this violent action, some of the king's officers learnt that the street leading to Wigan was not barricaded, nor were the houses possessed on that side. They presently entered that street with great bravery, pushing all before them. A regiment of foot were commanded upon this service and led by Lord Forrester. They marched up a straight passage behind the houses, and then halted until Lord Forrester came into the open street with his sword drawn to view how they were posted.

There were many shots fired at Lord Forrester, but unhurt he retired to his men, and then he came up again, marching at the head facing the barrier where Brigadier Mackintosh and his men were posted. They plied them with shot in a noble attempt to break through, but the rebels replied with ferocious fire upon them from houses at both sides of the street.

In consequence a number of that old and brave regiment were killed or wounded, Lord Forrester receiving many wounds. The foot soldiers fired smartly upon the rebels, but did little damage as they were generally covered from shot, while the rebels delivered many fatal shots securely.

Among their victims were two gallant gentlemen, one of which was Capt. Farquharson who was shot through the bone of the leg, enduring a great deal of torture from the surgeon who attended to the many wounded at the White Bull Inn. His leg was cut off by

The White Bull Inn, in the centre, was used to treat the wounded.

an unskilled butcher rather than a surgeon, and before he faded into death he took a glass of brandy, and uttered these words – 'Come lads, here is our master's health; though I can do no more, I wish you good success.'

The next barrier which was attacked was commanded by Lord Charles Murray. He behaved with becoming dignity and spirit; being vigorously attacked and not having sufficient numbers of men, he was reinforced by fifty gentlemen volunteers from the churchyard. The King's troops resolved to attack again, whereby Lord Charles gave orders to his men to receive them. Though the king's troops that made this attack were, for the major part raw and undisciplined, being newly enlisted men, they showed bravery and the excellent conduct of the experienced officers enabled them to engage in a furious fight. However, Lord Charles Murray maintained his post and obliged them to retreat with loss. A significant number were slain, some from the loop holes of the barn and other out-buildings, and others from fire from the barrier itself.

Hitherto the rebels seemed to have some great advantage, by having repulsed the king's troops in all their different attacks and maintained their posts. With night drawing on, no new action took place, and during all this time, and all Saturday night, Sunday, and a great portion of that night also, the king's forces kept playing incessant platoons, firing upon the rebels. They did not do much execution with all this platooning, although three were killed including a Highland gentleman.

There were several houses and barns set on fire, by both parties, for the express purpose of covering themselves amongst the smoke and dislodging men from their posts; so that if the wind had blown almost at any time from any quarter, the town of Preston would have been razed to the ground and the rebels would have been burnt to ashes within it. These skirmishes were a great means of the death of some, and the wounding of others, on both sides.

The third attack was at the Windmill, in the street that led towards Lancaster, where the barrier was defended by 300 men under the command of Mr Mackintosh, who along with his men behaved in the boldest manner possible. They made a terrific fire upon the king's forces, killing many instantly upon the spot and obliging them to make a retreat, which they did very quickly. Those captured assured the rebels they would die first rather than take up against his present Majesty, warning them that more forces were coming from all parts.

When General Carpenter arrived in Preston, with extra Dragoons, he received a full account of all that had taken place within the town, approving of what Gen. Willis had done. Finding that the major part of the horse and dragoons of the king's troops were posted on one side of the town, he brought them off in parties to several other posts.

Also, on viewing the ground near the river on the Penwortham side, to his surprise no troops were posted at that end of Fishergate, and consequently many rebels had escaped and rode off that way without a fight. At the upper end of this street there was another barricade with two cannons, but no attack had been made on this. Here Carpenter ordered two squadron of horse to patrol, in order to prevent any more rebels from fleeing and any that did were cut to pieces by the horse soldiers.

The rebels being surrounded on all sides were consequently blocked up in the town. Being sensible of their forlorn condition, and also being short of ammunition in order to make a stubborn resistance, they began to mediate amongst themselves on what must be done.

The Highlanders proposed that they would sally out and fall upon the king's troops, and by thus fighting their way, sword in hand, would be dying like men of honour; but they were overruled and not permitted to stir.

Gen. Willis was then prevailed upon by Lord Widdrington, Colonel Oxburgh, and some others with regards to a capitulation, flattering themselves that they would receive good terms from the king's officers. Col. Oxburgh stating that he had great acquaintance with some of them. In consequence of this, he offered to go out and treat of a surrender.

Col. Oxburgh went with the trumpet to Gen. Carpenter, who allowed him to go and come freely, but told him they might expect no other terms than to lay down their arms and submit to the king's mercy. He returned with this answer to the rebels and a second message was sent by them for some time to consider it.

About three o'clock in the afternoon Col. Cotton, with a dragoon and with a drum beating a cha-made before them, marched up Fishergate from Gen. Carpenter. He alighted at the sign of the Mitre, where the chiefs of the rebels were assembled together. He told them that he had come in order to receive a positive answer from them, and he was answered that serious debates were taking place within the Mitre Inn, betwixt the English and Scots, and if Gen. Carpenter would grant them a cessation of arms until the next morning about seven o'clock, they would be more able to settle the matter.

Upon this Col. Cotton sent the drum to beat a chamade before the doors of some houses where the king's men continued firing, to cause them to cease, and to await further orders from Gen. Carpenter. But the poor fellow was shot dead upon his horse, as he was beating his drum. Whether it was done by the king's men or whether it was done by a rebel was uncertain.

Rumours circulated among the rebels that terms had been granted them at this short treaty, which was to have secured their lives. Nonetheless, the common men were one and all against capitulation, and were terribly enraged when told of this, declaring they would rather die fighting. Their rage could not be quelled for a while, as they threatened one another, with one killed and several wounded.

Eventually they all submitted at seven o'clock in the morning of 14 November, and being disarmed were all secured and put into the power of the king's troops.

At last Generals Willis and Carpenter entered the town in due form, at the head of their troops. They came in with sound of trumpets and beat of drums, both parties meeting in the Market Place. Here the Highlanders stood drawn up with their arms: the lords, gentlemen, and officers were first secured and placed under guard in several rooms in the various inns, where they remained some time. The Highlanders laid down their arms in the place where they stood drawn up, and they were put into the church under a sufficient guard.

When all was deemed safe, with the rebels disarmed and secured, Gen. Carpenter seeing there was not sufficient room in the town for the number of men under his command sent some forces to Wigan, there to rest a day or two. The day following Gen. Carpenter and other officers departed Preston, and left the care of the prisoners to Gen. Willis whom he felt had the honour of victory upon his shoulders.

The beaten rebels surrendered
in the Market Place.

The first thing to be done was bury the slain of both sides. And then Gen. Willis
prepared to march also, but not before reflecting on the losses and the woundings
inflicted on the king's troops. There were reckoned to have been 200 of His Majesty's
forces killed and of the rebels there were seventeen killed. Those taken at Preston by
the capitulation numbered close to 1,500 including several gentlemen, officers and two
clergymen. The fate of some of those captured is revealed when we consider the grim
tales of Gallows Hill. Others though had to endure an equally gruesome end on Tower Hill
in London, among them James Radcliffe, Earl of Derwentwater who had been a childhood
companion of James Stuart. After being beheaded for treason a cast was made of his face.
His likeness is on display these days in the Harris Museum.

Grim Are The Tales of Gallows Hill

The present day site of the church of St Thomas of Canterbury and the English Martyrs is
a familiar landmark of our city on Garstang Road – yet the ground it stands on hides many
secrets of the areas past. On the northern side of the town, at the extreme corner of what
was known as Preston Moor, it was the very spot where men used to be hanged. Gallows

Hill as it was known is long associated with the 1715 Rebellion. Records show that at the height of the conflict sixteen rebels were hanged upon Gallows Hill, for high treason and conspiracy. Early in the following year forty-two condemned prisoners – said to be of all religions – were hanged and decapitated at Preston. Amongst those were five men familiar to Preston folk, namely Richard Shuttleworth, Roger Muncaster, Thomas Cowpe, William Butler and William Arkwright. The cost of putting them to death including erecting gallows, materials, hurdle, fire and cart to transport them was recorded as £12 0s 4d. This fee apparently included the then common practice of setting up the heads of the victims on poles in front of the town hall, or some other public place. Two executioners shared the grim task and they pocketed £7 between them to cover their journey by horse back and living expenses.

In 1817 when Gallows Hill was cut through, so that the great northern road to Lancaster might be improved, two coffins were discovered, and inside them were found two headless bodies. Also discovered were timbers that appeared to have been part of the gallows, and a brass hand axe was found not far from the coffins.

The foundation stone of the church was laid in May 1866, and the building was opened in December 1867. Of Gothic design, it cost £15,000 to build. Fittingly, many of the streets that grew up around English Martyrs church were given the names of those who had suffered in this conflict or other conflicts of those bloody and barbaric days.

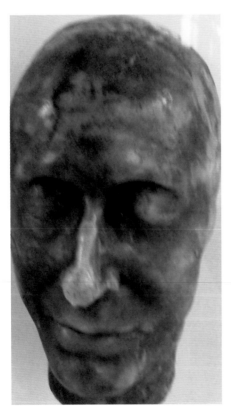

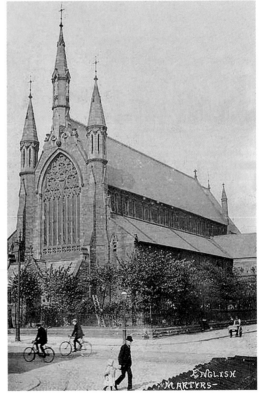

The death mask of James Radcliffe.

English Martyrs c. 1900 on site of Gallows Hill.

Arthur Devis and the Young Pretender

Fortunately in 1745 when the second Jacobite Rebellion took place most of it passed Preston by. This time there were skirmishes in the town but nothing so significant. James Darbyshire was the Mayor of Preston that year and Prince Charles Edward Stuart entered Preston on the 27 November, with an army of Highlanders, upwards of 300 in number, when a tax was laid upon the inhabitants for money and provisions. The prince appeared as a pedestrian, with the Highland dress, plaid, cocked hat, and a large peruke, and his sword by his side. The headquarters were the White Bull in Churchgate. When Bonnie Prince Charlie and his rebel forces proclaimed his father king in the Market Place, the crowds rejoiced. Unfortunately the Young Pretender's mission failed when he came up against the troops of George II further south.

On the 12 December the rebels, in their retreat to Scotland, again came to Preston and on the following morning proceeded on their journey. They had not been gone out of town four hours before HRH the Duke of Cumberland and senior officers passed through in pursuit.

Above left: the artist. *Above right*: the Young Pretender.

According to an old manuscript of the time, Arthur Devis, a member of the famous Preston family of painters, had a narrow escape. The following anecdote explains – 'As a young man Mr Devis was considered so like Charles Edward (the Young Pretender) that he was upon one occasion arrested and only not killed on the spot because the soldiers thought they would get a better reward if they took him alive'. Arthur protested quite vehemently and a slight hesitation in his speech only made the soldiers more certain they had the right man. Fortunately for Arthur, his friends eventually convinced the soldiers that their captor was a local artist and he was released. Feeling that he was no longer safe in the town, he immediately fled to London where his father had already gone. Arthur Devis had been born in Preston, where his family had a house and a joiner's shop on the site of the future Red Lion public house in Church Street. Double portrait miniatures in oil of Arthur Devis and Prince Charlie showed how closely the pair seemed to look alike.

City of Bones and Graveyards

The grim discoveries by workmen whilst digging in the Gallows Hill area of Preston in 1817 were typical of the finds that have taken place down the centuries. As recently as March 2007 the *Lancashire Evening Post* broke the story that workers on a city centre site had halted development after uncovering five coffins, experts describing it as a significant discovery. The find was thought to be a medieval burial ground – the remnants of the old Friary which stood in the Friargate area of Preston throughout much of the Middle Ages.

The discovery of artefacts and even bodies is nothing new during excavations in Preston. When Anthony Hewitson wrote his History of Preston in 1883 he recorded the many conflicts that had occurred down the centuries. In fact he went so far as to say that probably no town in England had been the scene of more military conflicts. Battles during the reign of Henry VIII, Cavalier and Roundhead troops settling desperate encounters and an important drama played out with rebels and royalty – all happening within the old Borough boundaries.

As such, it is perhaps unsurprising that when workmen start digging foundations for new developments, they unearth coffins, skeletons and artefacts from centuries ago. Perhaps we should say 'digger beware' when any excavations are undertaken because many an unsuspecting workman has uncovered a glimpse of the past.

Friargate and the roads leading off it have been the scene of many a skirmish and, in 1810, workers digging at the rear of the Sun Inn unearthed a cartload of bones believed to have been those of soldiers who perished in the fighting of 1715. Amongst them was the skeleton of a man described as a giant of his day, being over 6 feet 7 inches tall and with a sword in his right hand.

At different periods within the nineteenth century numerous relics of the civil wars' memorable struggle of 1648 have been discovered in the locality of the battle. Several iron cannon-balls have from time to time been picked up on farm land at Fulwood. Several bullets were found in 1856 in the immediate neighbourhood of the site in Ribbleton.

When the Strawberry Garden, near Walton Bridge, was first laid out, several coins and human remains were found. Two cannonballs, weighing between eight and nine pounds each, were later found close to Darwen Bridge. Bullets have also been found on Walton Flats together with a sword and a small dagger, with the initials O.C. 1648 engraved upon it. Also discovered was an identical boot to those worn by Oliver Cromwell and his body of men. Historian Peter Whittle also recorded that a gentleman residing near Fulwood Moor had, whilst making a hole in the floor of his house, discovered a little below the surface, a quantity of silver coins of various sizes. They consisted of those of Edward IV, nearly defaced; Charles I, James I, and Elizabeth I, in a fine state of preservation; also a coin of Philip IV of Spain.

In addition there were numerous graveyards within the old borough boundaries prior to the opening of Preston Cemetery in July 1855. Some remain, whilst others have had the corpses moved to Preston Cemetery. The graveyard of Christ Church in Bow Lane was opened in 1838 and 155 burials took place there. In 1971 when the old church site was redeveloped the bodies were re-interred in Preston Cemetery.

Preston Cemetery, the last resting place of many local folk.

One of the major relocation exercises came in 2003, when almost 2,000 bodies were removed from the derelict graveyard of St Augustine's church in Avenham as building work was undertaken for the new sports centre.

In the news in May 2009 was the area of Fox Street that was for many years the graveyard of St Wilfred's, and is now a place to park your car. Planners preparing a report for the building of a Premier Inn close by were reminded of the car parks significant past. It being a place where not only Roman Catholics of old were buried, but also victims of the cholera epidemic that swept the town.

Likewise, you can park your car on the site of the old Trinity church and graveyard once known as Patten Field. The church had an excellent walled burial ground with northern and southern entrances graced by ornamental square Gothic pillars. Only the steps into the old graveyard and two stone pillars tell the tale of the past.

In the heart of the city the old parish church graveyard of St John's has been subject to much change in recent decades with many monuments moved and grave slabs repositioned. A reminder of that dreadful malady, typhus fever, is recorded in the fact that upwards of fifty victims were laid to rest in this graveyard in December 1813. And of course centuries earlier when the plague struck Preston countless victims were also buried there.

During the period from 1663 to 1682, when the Revd Seth Bushell was vicar of Preston the Court Leet records showed that the graveyard of the parish church was in a poor state.

St George's chapel and graveyard; a nineteenth-century view.

In 1665 nine persons were brought to account for allowing their pigs to roam the grounds in an unChristian manner. Seven years later the walls and fences were in a better state, but the churchyard was described as being in a disorderly, unseemly condition; human bones from graves being scattered about the surface.

The St George's chapel graveyard, a place many noteworthy Preston folk were buried, bears little resemblance today to its appearance decades ago. Renovation work has led to the removal of some significant memorials and gravestones.

Then there is the graveyard of St Peter's church in Fylde Road that these days is at the heart of the university campus. Part of the original graveyard remains undisturbed, including the last resting place of Richard 'Dicky' Turner, the reformed drunkard who coined the phrase 'teetotal' to the delight of the temperance movement.

Meanwhile, the St Paul's graveyard on Ringway, with its crumbling monuments, is at the very heart of radio land, with the church building being home to the tuneful melodies of Rock FM. This was the burial place of many cholera victims.

Not far from this site if you head towards Church Street, was the Unitarian chapel erected in 1717 which is now at the heart of a development of apartments. This place had a small graveyard where a number of notable worshippers were buried.

At the site of St Walburge's church, as they dug the foundations in 1836, workers came across the old Magdalen burial grounds of thirteenth-century origins. Five skeletons were unearthed and a mass of human bones, along with a stone coffin. There are many other examples of monuments and gravestones that have moved or been rearranged down the years.

A present-day view of St George's chapel with cars where graves were once dug.

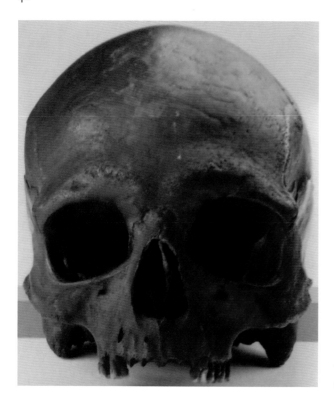

The oldest male skull discovered during the Docks excavations.

During the excavations necessary to create the 40-acre Preston Docks site a number of interesting discoveries were made. In June 1886 it was reported that the workmen had come upon an old weir and unearthed two dugout canoes, and a large amount of animal remains, mostly of oxen, along with a unique collection of human skull remains. The human skulls have ever since been of great interest locally and a number of them are now on display in the Harris Museum. They have been analysed in recent times and conclusions drawn from carbon dating are that the oldest male skull is of a Stone Age man of some 5,500 years ago who died when about forty years old. Older still is a skull of an elderly woman who lived about 6,000 years ago.

It is little surprise, therefore, given the number of burial grounds and ancient sites in Preston that down the years the toiling workmen will uncover the remains of the souls of centuries before, be they either victims of some conflict of long ago or simply been laid to rest at the end of their days.

Perhaps the most fitting way to end this chapter is to recall the former Preston businessman James Todd, who lived at Farington Lodge. An accountant by trade, he was a millionaire director of several companies. He travelled worldwide during his lifetime on business matters, but maintained a keen affection for his offices in Winckley Square. So much so that his last request was to be cremated and his ashes put in an urn and placed in the wall of that building. There they remain to this today behind a brick that is engraved simply 'J. T. 1863–1931'.

Cremation was a rarity in those days, with the nearest crematorium in Manchester. The Preston Crematorium was only opened in late January 1962.

James Todd died in 1931.

Doctor, Doctor – Quacks & Cures

Down the centuries Preston has had many notable medical men who all played their part in the establishment of the health service of today. Long gone are the days when patients were bled, cupped, and leeched and given brandy or whisky to kill the pain. In consequence, life expectancy has increased beyond all expectations due to the advances in medical science.

Fortunately, long gone are the days like those of 1894 when the Medical Officer of Health for Preston gave his report to the Sanitary Committee and stated that over 2,000 folk had died that year from the likes of consumption, bronchitis, inflammation of the lungs, diarrhoea, whooping cough and scarlet fever. In fact the town with a population of 111,425 was second in the death rate table behind Liverpool. Indeed, only seventy-six residents of the town had survived long enough to have old age as the reason for their demise entered on their death certificate.

One noted physician and poet born in Preston in 1641 was Dr Edward Baynard. He was one of the earliest exponents of the use of cold bathing for good health. After spending most of his childhood in Preston he went to London, to the plague riddled capital of 1655. Having survived that horror he went to Holland where he studied for his medical degree, returning to England to eventually become a Fellow of the Royal College of Physicians.

Dr Baynard was no stranger to the Black Death.

In between he often made visits to Preston of various length. In fact, his daughter Ann, who was something of a prodigy, was born here in 1672. In a book on health Edward Baynard wrote: 'I remember when I lived in Preston, in Lancashire, a man died with a cheese in his belly – by drinking new milk upon stale beer; which so frightened people from the use of milk, that all forsook it, but the wiser calves; another died from a surfeit of salmon, after which accident some would never more touch salmon.'

Ann Baynard who was carefully trained by her father in philosophy, mathematics, astronomy, physics and literature was said at the age of twenty-three to have arrived at the knowledge of a bearded philosopher. Sadly she died just a couple of years later.

A leading physician in eighteenth-century Preston was Dr Richard Shepherd who resided in a house on Friargate. In the gardens at the back of his home he cultivated herbs with which to treat his patients. He became an influential member of local society and was twice elected Mayor of Preston. A kindly man, he had a great passion for books and when he died in 1761 he left his valuable library to the town.

One of the town's most prominent physicians from the latter part of the seventeenth century was William St Claire who arrived in Preston after studying in Edinburgh. He built up an extensive practice and was also surgeon to the local militia. An accomplished horseman, he had patients as far away as Yorkshire who he would visit on a weekly basis. He was a pioneering medical practitioner with large premises on Fishergate and served the town for close on forty years, dying in 1822, aged seventy.

In October 1809 a public dispensary was opened in Everton Gardens, the purpose being the relief of the sick and infirm poor. This charitable organisation tended patients that were recommended by the civic leaders, clergymen and benefactors. In its first decade no less than 16,000 people were cared for by the dispensary, which by then had moved to Fishergate.

Besides the dispensary there was a House of Recovery opened near to Trinity Church in June 1813. The main purpose of this facility was to prevent the spread of contagious diseases, a constant source of concern to town dwellers. This establishment was proud to

Dr Richard Shepherd, an early physician.   Dr William St Claire served the town well.

report in 1819 that 102 patients had been admitted, of which ninety-nine had been cured and discharged and three remained in care.

Certainly medical cures came at a cost and in 1823 the issue of leeches was high on the agenda. The cost of one leech had risen to three pence and strict rules were drawn up with regard to their use, use of the blood-sucking worm for bloodletting treatment being restricted to a month for each patient.

The need for a new House of Recovery to match the rising population led to the building of premises in Deepdale, where the future Preston Royal Infirmary would stand. This was opened in 1832, just in time to cope with an outbreak of smallpox, some 3,000 patients being treated of which 170 died. That year saw many places visited by the dreaded scourge cholera but Preston was unaffected. However, in 1848 the town was not so lucky with several cases reported, the first victim being a man in his late forties who lived in a cellar in Vicar Street. August 1849 was a particular harrowing time when six victims, all in the Bleasdale Street area of town, died within a week. The *Preston Guardian* described the cholera as a health inspector no man can misunderstand visiting – as it did – the undrained city, the uncleaned street, the cellar and the attic. Only around that time was it realised that drinking water was the main source of the infection.

Just prior to the Preston Guild of 1822 a young apothecary called Thomas Monk had begun medical practice in the town. Eager to advance local healthcare he worked long and hard, becoming a familiar figure with his involvement in political matters. A fitting reward for his services to the town was his selection as Mayor of the Borough in 1851.

The statute of Robert Peel in Winckley Square
unveiled by Dr Monk, who had his name removed after
conviction.

However, a few years later the town was stunned to hear Doctor Thomas Monk accused of forging the will of a dying patient. In some circles it was claimed he had poisoned the elderly man but no proof was forthcoming. Eventually he stood trial at Lancaster Castle accused of forgery and a guilty verdict led to him being sentenced to 'Penal Servitude for Life'. The convicted sixty-one-year-old was on his way to London's Millbank Penitentiary still protesting his innocence. After serving ten years hard labour he was released on a ticket of leave and returned to Preston to resume his medical practice. Still a well-liked man, he was appointed physician to the Preston Oddfellows. His sentence was finally revoked in 1880 and he lived to be almost ninety – dying in 1888.

By 1870 the House of Recovery had been upgraded thanks to generous benefactors and the title Preston & County of Lancaster Royal Infirmary was adopted. Shortly afterwards the old Dispensary in Fishergate was closed and amalgamated into the new Infirmary.

In the middle of the nineteenth century Robert Charles Brown returned to Preston after completing his medical studies in London. The newly qualified surgeon was to play a prominent role in the town's health service, starting as he did with daily surgeries at the Preston Dispensary. He soon became actively involved with the new Infirmary. They were difficult days with crude methods and primitive equipment. Patients often being doped with opium, or intoxicated with alcohol, prior to surgery.

In the days prior to the opening of the Infirmary Dr Brown had often tended to those injured on the railways in the nearest beer house. The amputation of a limb, or other drastic surgery was carried out in appalling conditions, often by candlelight. Eager to see the Infirmary resources improved, Dr Brown often funded

Above: The Preston Royal Infirmary grew from the House of Recovery.

Right: Dr Robert Charles Brown, a dedicated man.

equipment from his own purse, a new operating theatre at a cost of £2,700 being such an example. In his later years he penned a book called *Sixty Four Years A Doctor* which chronicled his days as a leading local surgeon and gave a glimpse of life in his Winckley Square home.

A knighthood and Freedom of The Borough were just rewards for 'Preston's Grand Old Man' who was born in the town in 1836 and who died in November 1925. At the reading of his will it was revealed that two thirds of his £80,000 fortune would go to local hospitals.

In 1904 the Preston Royal Infirmary, due once more to the generosity of Dr Charles Brown, opened an up-to-date X-ray department. Put in charge was Dr Arthur Ernest Raynor, the son of a physician, who had studied medicine in Manchester. From his early twenties he was in local practice and dealing with accident victims. On one occasion he was called out to a back street dwelling where a patient was near to death with a gangrenous leg. Dr Raynor chloroformed the man beneath the light of an oil lamp and cut off his leg with a knife. The outcome of the harrowing experience was the saving of the patient's life. The X-ray equipment was a great aid, enabling treatment for previously hopeless cases.

Around this time Dr Raynor's sister Edith Rigby was very much in the local news. She was a well-known campaigner for the Preston Suffragette movement with their slogan of 'Votes For Women'.

However, when the First World War broke out the ladies put aside their grievances and worked for the war effort. Dr Raynor also showed his patriotism by serving in the Middle East as an Army medic.

During the war years the hospital facilities were stretched and a temporary hospital was set up on Moor Park, the pre-fabricated buildings being used for the convalescence of wounded servicemen.

Once the war was over, Dr Raynor was back at the Infirmary working long hours and tending to the sick. He was a great believer in psychiatry, often being heard to say, 'Make them believe the medicine works and it does.' Dr Raynor was a remarkable character and was still administering X-ray treatment in his eighties.

Medically, things have progressed greatly in the city, the new Royal Preston hospital opened in 1981 being testament to that. No doubt the present century will provide many more people who will earn a place in the city's history for their contribution to medical matters.

The walking wounded at Moor Park hospital in 1917.

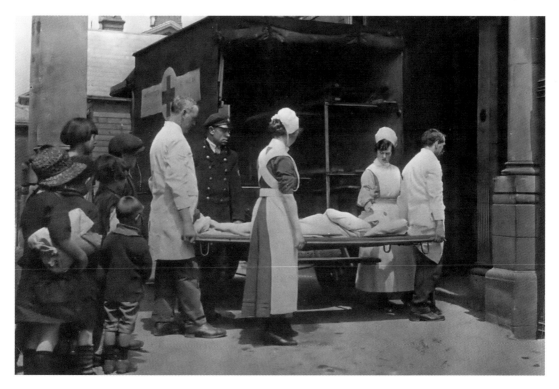

A patient arrives at Preston Royal Infirmary in 1923 for emergency treatment, watched by curious onlookers.

The Plague of Preston

We know that Preston did not escape the awful consequences of the Plague or Black Death that ravaged the whole country over a long period, especially in the fourteenth and seventeenth centuries. There is documentary evidence that Preston was visited by the Plague, the greatest calamity that ever hit our island, in 1349–50, 1466 and 1630–1.

In the middle of the fourteenth century the county suffered very severely from the effects of this pestilence with it recorded that within the Hundred of Amounderness over 13,000 people are said to have died from it between September 1349 and January 1350. The two towns which lost the greater number were Kirkham and Preston, in each of which 3,000 folk are reported to have died. Poverty was certainly prevalent at the time with records showing that only about 500 of the Preston victims had an estate of £5 or more, and of those only 300 had made a will. The roll call of the dead included William Mirreson and his wife, Thomas Marshall and his wife, Robert Litester, John Tilleson

The graveyard at the rear of Preston parish church (now St John's Minster) where countless souls were buried.

and William Wrotchol. Records also show that towards the close of the year 1349 the chapel of the hospital of Mary Magdalen was closed, and so remained for eight weeks in consequence of the ravages made by the Black Death.

And we do have detailed information on the latter visitation that can be found in the registers of the parish church. The year 1630 contains the following significant entry – 'Here beginneth the visitation of Almighty God, the Plague.' Nothing more than this bold statement; the rest of the terrible story is told by the rapidly increasing number of burials as the dreadful months passed by.

In November there were ten burials, and then those pathetic happenings continued to increase in number, until July, of the following year, the number reaches the appalling total of 321, whilst in the previous year there were only three burials in July. The 321 burials is a frightful record for one month. For the calendar year 1631 the total recorded funerals were 951 – a frightening statistic even though the parish church was the only burial ground in the town.

Husbands and wives, parents and children, masters and servants, were victims and often buried on the same day, or rapidly following each other to the grave. In some cases whole families seem to have been contaminated; no less than one third of the population were affected in the 12 months that the epidemic lasted. Not a single marriage was solemnised during the same period as fear and uncertainty reigned.

The trauma recorded in the parish church register is confirmed in the Guild Order Book of the period with the following entry:

The great sickness of the Plague and Pestilence wherein the number of eleven hundred persons and upwards dyed within the town and parish of Preston, began about the tenth day of November 1630, and continued the space of one whole year next after.

Signed William Preston, Mayor of Preston.

One familiar figure of those plague-infested days in Preston was William Lemon, who was the Mayor of Preston in 1624 and 1633. He was the owner of the Alms Houses in St John's Wynd called Lemon's Alms Houses, and it is recorded that his father was a victim of the plague and was buried in late August 1631. Fortunately, normality returned in 1632 with just thirty-nine burials recorded.

The Black Death was mainly a rat-borne disease, transmitted from rat to rat, and from rat to man, by the bite of rat fleas. It was the day of the black rat, rife in the wooden framework buildings filled in with clay and plaster. The Plague was one of the most infectious and deadly diseases of those early days and many methods were adopted to keep towns free from infection. People fled from infected districts hoping to find some place free from the scourge, but they often carried the germs and fleas with them. Town authorities took precautions against entry and the regulations were harsh. Citizens were forbidden to visit the markets and fairs of infected towns. London was recognised as the chief source of the infection and even the first parliament of Charles I's reign at Westminster was adjourned to Oxford, because the Plague was raging in the London.

The outfit of a brave doctor visiting the Plague victims.

Among other causes, foul air from moors and fens, standing water and sewage, and multitudes of people living in small dwellings uncleanly kept, were blamed for the terrible epidemics. For the purification of houses, or personal preventive, vinegar was regarded as the sovereign remedy.

According to the physicians of the day – 'They who are infected are cold without, hot within, are heavy, weary and lumpish; have great pain in the head, sadness of the mind, sleepiness, loss of appetite, thirst, vomiting, dryness of the mouth.' The preventions they recommended included leaves of carduss, butterbur roots, rhinoceros blood and hide boiled in sorrel water.

St Walburge's church at Maudland. This was the area where the Chapel of the Lepers was believed to be sited centuries ago.

A carved stone figure and a holy water stoop (now housed in the Harris Museum) are both relics of the days when the Grey Friars walked and prayed on the streets of Preston.

The Hospital of the Lepers

Leprosy in the twelfth and thirteenth centuries found many victims in the northern parts of Lancashire and those who did not find shelter in one of the hospitals piously founded for their benefit, appear to have not only been outcasts but were treated with cruelty and abuse.

Not being allowed to live in the large towns they found shelter in the neighbourhood forests, but even there they were often not allowed to rest in peace. This fact is clearly proved by a writ of 1220, addressed to the sheriff of the county, instructing him to see that the lepers were no longer molested, but that in future their beasts and herds were to pasture in the forests of Lancashire, from whence they were also to be allowed to take firewood and timber for the building of their huts.

In the reign of Henry II at least three Hospitals for Lepers had been founded in the north of Lancashire: in Coniston, at Lancaster, and St Mary Magdalene at Preston, the exact date of the foundation of the latter is unknown, but it was an established hospital in the time period 1154–89.

In the middle of the fourteenth century it was recorded how pilgrims from various parts of the country made visits to this Chapel of the Lepers, particularly on the principal feast days of the year, and on the feast day of St Mary Magdalene in July. The tenants of the lands and tenements of the hospital in the fifteenth century paid homage and service to the Cliftons of Kirkham.

After the ravages of the Dissolution of the Monastries, ordered by Henry VIII between 1536 and 1541, the hospital and chapel were in much decay and ruin and a number of disputes took place as to the use of the pasture lands that surrounded it. Such a dispute occurred in 1545 when James Walton complained in the Duchy Court that in May he had put thirteen head of cattle into one of his leased closes of land near the hospital, and that one William Whalley and others not only impounded them but had proceeded to pull down the building of the Free Chapel, which contained six or seven chambers, and also carried away the timber and stones belonging thereto and one of the bells, besides relics, and other adornments belonging to the chapel. Thomas Barlow, the last incumbent of the Free Chapel, was allowed to retire with a pension of £5 a year. The Hospital for Lepers no doubt fell into disuse long before the chapel was allowed to come into the state in which it was in 1542.

The exact position of the building is unclear, except it was believed to be somewhere between the present day church of St Walburge's and the old Talbot School in the Maudland area of the town.

The Old Monastery of Grey Friars

Just beyond the north side of Fishergate where railway coaches rumble past daily, once stood a monastery. The secret life of the Grey Friars is buried deep within the town's history, although long gone in 1820 it was described by Preston historian Peter Whittle as thus -'The Grey Friars' house would in its time of splendour and glory, accommodate the proudest monarch; was built in a style of Gothic magnificence, including within its walls apartments for upwards of 500 monks.'

In the grounds were orangeries, greenhouses and ornamental flower beds decorated with statuary and columns brought from afar. It is evident it must have been a beautiful spot in the lovely undulating valley which formerly sloped from Fishergate Hill outside the borders of our ancient borough. From thither daily up Friary Lane into Friargate grey robed friars passed along on their errands of mercy amongst the sick and poor of the town.

The monastery was founded in 1221 by Edmund, Earl of Lancaster, and became a place of considerable importance. It was disbanded at the Dissolution of the Monasteries in 1536–41 and afterwards a considerable portion of the building was pulled down. What remained was converted into a private dwelling where an influential man named Oliver Breres, Mayor of Preston in 1558, and his descendants lived for quite some time. By 1614 the buildings had been converted to a house of correction – this establishment being referred to in 1682 by Dr Kuerdon in a mischievous way as follows:

A little more remote from the town stands the ruins of an ancient Priory, formerly built for the relief of begging fryers – called the Grey Friars; but what is left thereof now standing is employed as a House of Correction for the country's use, to keep in safety and at hard work the likes of vagabonds, rogues, thieves, and sturdy beggars. Those of dissolute behaviour are under a strict master, with slender diet and whipping chair at hand.

It was later visited by prison reformer Dr Howard who severely condemned its conditions, leading to the building of the Stanley Street gaol in 1789.

The Preston–Lancaster Canal, constructed in 1798, passed through the spacious grounds behind the monastery and speculation is that many large stones from the ruins were used in the building of the coal wharves of the canal. In the grounds there was also a famous well; the water it contained was believed to have health-giving properties. It was known as the Lady Well and after the canal had been built it was still a place of pilgrimage for the faithful who drank its waters. During the cutting of the canal, several remains were unearthed, including a leaden conduit pipe branching from the Lady Well, a number of coins and some bones, sad remnants of mortality. Although now buried beneath our city, its existence is recalled by Ladywell Street.

Subsequently, the old monastery building was made into dwelling houses and some of them survived into the early nineteenth century when they were described as filthy. Then it was turned into a cotton factory for a time and later was used as a barracks for militia purposes. Ultimately parts of it, and some of the walls, were incorporated into Stevenson's foundry, Lower Pitt Street. These premises were demolished with the remaining portions of the old monastery when the main railway line outside Preston Station to the north was widened in the late nineteenth century. The old sun dial that was on an outer wall of the monastery was bought by a gentleman from Manchester to hang in his garden.

The appropriate naming of Barracks Street, off Marsh Lane, gave us a clue as to the approximate position where the monastery stood, but this street no longer exists since the building of the new International Hotel on Marsh Lane.

The new Preston International Hotel on the old Grey Friars grounds – the stone wall of the old canal bridge remains on Marsh Lane.

The Orphans and the Sisters of Mercy

In early 2009 there was a fire at the old St Joseph's Nursing Home between Mount Street and Theatre Street, and later news broke that the nuns were about to leave the city. It brought into focus the derelict and neglected buildings that were once at the centre of the town's care for poor and sick alike.

If you are an old Prestonian and wander down Mount Street these days you will stumble upon a depressing sight as you see before you the locked shutters and boarded windows of premises that were once Mount Street Hospital. Continue your trek into the parallel thoroughfare that is Theatre Street and at the bottom you will come upon the locked gates of the old St Joseph's Orphanage with broken panes, boarded doors and barbed wire on top of the gates. It is a sorry state for premises that were for many years at the very centre of a caring local community.

The orphanage was built in 1872 solely for the purpose of providing for orphaned Roman Catholic girls. It was built thanks mainly to the charity of a local Catholic lady, Maria Holland, and the children were generally instructed and looked after by nuns. Within a decade the building had been extended thanks to the generosity of the Catholic community and over fifty girls reaped the benefits at one time.

Maria Holland, a great benefactor recorded in stone.

By 1877 more funds were provided by the elderly benefactor Maria Holland, who was the wealthy widow of James Holland, a tallow chandler, for the erection of 'St. Joseph's Institute for the Sick Poor' and it opened its doors in 1879, shortly before she died at her home in Bushell Place. The hospital was to be run by the Dutch order of nuns of the 'Sisters of Charity of our Lady Mother of Mercy', who also ran the St Joseph's Orphanage. It was intended for the less fortunate in the local Catholic community and its running costs were funded by voluntary contributions with local medical gentlemen providing their services for free.

In 1884 a small cottage next to the hospital in Mount Street was purchased and two rooms were opened up as accommodation for private patients. Soon after, funds were raised to build a small chapel and by 1909 a fully equipped operating theatre was in use and from the beginning the operations were all recorded as successful, a true testimony to the care taken by the surgeons and hospital staff.

The work of the hospital that became known affectionately as 'Mount Street Hospital' steadily increased and by the time of the outbreak of the First World War a fully working men's ward had been added. The sisters were anxious to assist the war effort and they offered the ward to the government for the use of soldiers. Within weeks a dozen wounded Belgian soldiers were on the ward and a steady stream of soldiers followed as the conflict dragged on. Local volunteers were plentiful and the soldiers were generously supplied with clothing, food and entertainment during their stay in the hospital by those eager to help.

Soon after the war the hospital was equipped with X-ray equipment and many alterations were made in the orphanage and the hospital. The children were educated in the orphanage by the sisters until 1932 at which time they began to attend St Wilfred's Primary School.

By 1933 a wing was added to the hospital with a surgical ward, maternity and labour wards, as well as private rooms. Once again during the Second World War wounded servicemen were taken in, many of them Dutch and Belgian sailors. A little later the hospital was recognised as a training school for state-enrolled nurses, accepting its first trainees in 1945, and it gained much recognition for its training methods.

The hospital continued to progress post-war and in 1958 a ward block was added at a cost of £80,000 for treating the chronic sick and to provide beds for geriatric patients under the NHS.

Unfortunately the maternity unit, where many a Prestonian had been brought into the world, was forced to close in 1966 because of rising costs and a shortage of midwives. What joy had come from this place as the mothers cradled their newly born infants.

As for the orphanage, the number of children in care decreased considerably by 1960 and eventually the trustees decided that a home for orphans was no longer necessary. The few remaining children were found foster homes and the orphanage rooms were converted into accommodation for nurses.

However, by the time the hospital celebrated its centenary it was a 120-bed hospital and an operating theatre for joint surgery had been added at a cost of £30,000. It was one of the few private hospitals remaining in the North-West and for a while it flourished following the closure of the private wing of Preston Royal Infirmary. At the time of the

Baby boom days with Sister Winefride and nurses.

centenary celebrations there were twenty-three Sisters of Mercy in Preston with six of them working in the hospital and three of them working as midwives in the community. The superior of the local community Sister Anne Marie was born in Preston and had entered the Order in 1946. Sister Winefride, with thirty-nine years' service at the hospital, was the matron and she was proud to announce that thirty pupil nurses were under her tuition, all destined for a life in the religious order.

After a further decade of caring, the hospital was delivered a blow when it was announced that the NHS would not be renewing their contract for the use of seventy-eight beds at St Joseph's Hospital. The charity trust that ran the hospital soon hit a financial crisis and after part of the hospital was closed off and up to thirty staff made redundant, the inevitable full closure came early in 1987. It seems like Mount Street's years of caring are definitely over because early in 2003 even the Mount Street Nursing Home that opened after the hospital closure had to admit defeat in its battle for survival.

When the hospital closed back in 1987, the Charity Commissioners were hoping for a quick disposal of the premises. It is now almost thirty years and various planning applications later, yet the future of this historic site still seems to be in the balance. Even the advertising hoarding displaying futuristic apartments is now overgrown by ivy and with each passing year the decaying buildings look even more forlorn. Just another example of our architectural heritage being left to rot.

A view from Mount Street of the decaying hospital building.

Broken window panes amid the derelict structure.

A view from Theatre Street of the old orphanage building.

Tulketh Hall – Going, Going, Gone!

In late May 1959, residents of the Tulketh area of town witnessed the final reckoning for one of Preston's most famous halls. Tulketh Hall, previously described as one of the most stately homes of old England, was being reduced to rubble. The building had stood empty for eighteen months – a weathering hulk, its walls cracked, its timbers riddled with woodworm, its many windows shattered by children.

Once a monastery, later the home of aristocracy, in more recent times an industrial school and an army records office, the hall was being sacrificed to industrial progress. According to a *Lancashire Evening Post* reporter who visited the site, demolition had been rapid and already the building was roofless, soon the castellated turrets would disappear, then the walls and within a month the ancient monument would be levelled to dust.

The final days for Tulketh Hall, once surrounded by countryside and situated on a steep hill in the Hesketh Street/Tulketh Crescent area of Ashton.

Nobody knows exactly when the original structure was built, but in the latter half of the nineteenth century it was restored by Joseph Hansom, the much admired architect and the inventor of the Hansom cab. Apparently an order of monks found their way to Preston and founded a monastery at Tulketh in 1124. Their stay was but a short one with them moving to Barrow in 1127 to establish Furness Abbey. The Travers family took over the hall and were succeeded by the Werdens and they in turn succeeded by the Rawstornes. Eventually in 1687 the hall was acquired by the Heskeths of North Meols. Robert Hesketh, who was Mayor of Preston in 1757/8, is credited with improving the building around that time, including the creation of its castellated appearance.

It was later occupied by George Edmondson, an educationalist and well known Quaker. The Revd T. Johnson the incumbent of St Mark's church resided there later, as did a cotton manufacturer and gold thread manufacturer.

The Brothers of Charity took over the place in 1898 and used it as an industrial school until the outbreak of the First World War. After the war they turned it into a training centre for young students of their brotherhood. The Diocese of Lancaster bought the premises just before the Second World War for teaching purposes and the next occupants were the Army who rented the building as their records office.

A secret underground passage between Tulketh Hall and Penwortham Priory was rumoured to exist, but this has never been found.

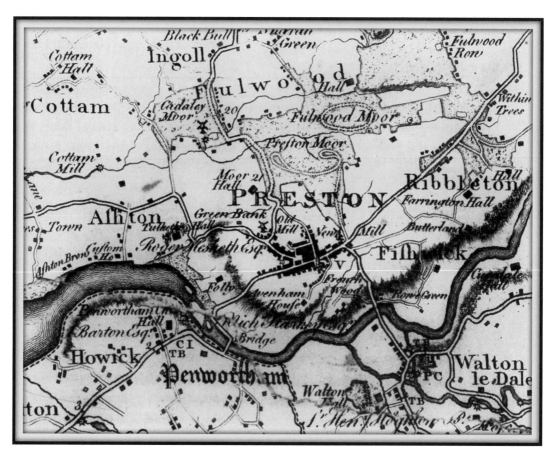

Yates' map of Preston in 1786 showing a number of halls – including Ribbleton & Tulketh Halls.

The Grand Hall of Ribbleton

The latest generations of Preston folk in the Ribbleton district have grown up with just the foundations to view of one of Preston's once grandest houses. This building was a significant landmark in its day and the residents therein left a legacy of Victorian life.

In truth it was not an ancient building, but was near the site of a much older one, which was the residence of John, second son of the Sherbornes of Stonyhurst, who purchased the manor in 1559. After his death his widow married her relative, William Ethelston, of Elston, but the manor remained in the Sherborne family until 1656. It was then sold to a Richard King, whose descendants sold it to Thomas Birchall at the beginning of the

Ribbleton Hall, an early twentieth-century postcard view.

A glimpse inside Ribbleton Hall.

nineteenth century, and it was his son, also named Thomas, who built the Ribbleton Hall of 1865 origins.

This Thomas Birchall, solicitor, who was Mayor of Preston in 1847/8, pulled down the old mansion and built a more fashionable and commodious residence a short distance away. Birchall, who was a clerk of the peace for Lancashire for upwards of forty years, was a senior partner in the family firm of solicitors and having acquired considerable wealth embarked on rebuilding his Ribbleton Hall home. The new larger Gothic-style mansion had fourteen bedrooms, five entertaining rooms, a drawing room, billiard room, conservatory, vine and peach houses and stables within the 65-acre site. He carried the title of colonel due to his voluntary role as a commander of the corps of artillery in the town. He had been married to Mary Rothwell since 1834, but their marriage was childless. Unbeknown to his wife Colonel Birchall had been having a love affair with a Preston woman, who he had provided with a furnished lodge in Manchester. This woman bore him a son and later she died giving birth to a daughter. Birchall then engaged another woman to look after his children, and in due course she became his mistress.

Early in May 1878 the town was shocked to hear of his sudden death whilst in Manchester on business. Only after his funeral at the reading of the will did his wife learn of Thomas Birchall's double life and the changes he had made leaving money in favour of his mistress and children. A long legal battle followed and eventual out of court settlements.

Widowed Mary Birchall remained at Ribbleton Hall until her death over twenty years later, at which time the mansion was rented to Nicholas Le Gendre Starkie who remained there for many years. Around 1926 it was sold to Mr George Moorcroft, who converted the Hall into apartments. During the Second World War it was requisitioned by the government for billeting American troops and after the troops departed it was purchased by Preston Corporation.

The new owners neglected the premises and it led to a visit by local historian John H. Spencer in May 1945. He wrote of his visit in the *Preston Herald*. What he found was a decaying and desolate sight that had been vandalised and become a playground for children intent on destruction. All the window panes were broken, the doors had been torn from their hinges and puddles of rain water covered the tiled floors. Everything in view was going to rack and ruin, loose and broken tiles, plaster peeling from walls, rotting wood and fractured pipes gave a scene of desolation. He saw them as the long lingering death throes and so they were.

By 1955 the house had been demolished and a public park was laid out named Grange Park which boasted a bowling green, pavilion, tennis courts, magnificent rose beds, as well as the numerous original trees and shrubs.

Unfortunately, thirty years on the park fell into decline and eventually work began in 1999 to restore the park to former glory. Excavation of the original foundations of Ribbleton Hall enabled the recreation of a floor plan of the layout of the building and conservatory, and the adjacent kitchen garden, thus enabling a glimpse of the Victorian splendour.

In Grange Park – a footprint of the past.

When the Canal Came Up To Town

Any visitors to Preston nowadays may find it hard to believe that the Lancaster Canal used to come all the way into town. In truth many tell-tale signs still remain. The curious names of public houses such as the old Watering Trough, the Ship Inn and the Lamb and Packet are all relevant to the days of that waterway, as is Aqueduct Street and Wharf Street.

The Lancaster Canal that served Preston from the dawn of the nineteenth century was an essential mode of transportation for people and for goods. It was the brainchild of engineer John Rennie and his intention was to transport goods between Wigan and Kendal.

Construction got under way in 1792 with work being carried out by gangs of navvies, equipped with spades, picks and wheelbarrows who toiled ten hours each day for a shilling. After digging the canal it had to be lined with clay to make it watertight, this was packed down hard either by the feet of the navvies or by driving cattle along its length.

The canal was opened between Preston and Tewitfield, in Westmorland, in 1797. It was quite an engineering feat in its day with 114 road and occupation bridges and two road aqueducts along its length. The waterway was a wonder of its time and its usefulness was extended when, in 1802, a tramway connection was established from the basin near

The old engine house on the Avenham incline.

to Wharf Street, in Preston to the summit at Bamber Bridge and onwards to link up with the Leeds and Liverpool Canal. The tramway consisted of two lines and its distance from the heart of Preston to Walton Summit was about five miles. Only wagons ran on it with eight or nine constituting a train.

Each train was drawn by two or three horses along the entire way except for the portion traversing Avenham Brow on the Preston side of the River Ribble. The wagons were drawn up or let down this very steep slope by a stationary engine that was in a building near to where the Belvedere now stands on Avenham Park.

For almost sixty years this method of transporting coal and limestone on the canals was continued. The last driver of the horses on the tramway was John Proctor who carried out the task for more than thirty years. Twice a day, he went from Preston to Walton Summit, partly walking and partly riding. He did so much walking that records reveal it was necessary for him to have his clogs resoled weekly.

There had of course been ambitious plans to replace the tramway with an aqueduct over the River Ribble, but financial difficulties meant the tramway was never replaced and the original wooden tram bridge was left to serve the purpose of crossing the river. Despite the fact that the Preston to Kendal canal had fewer locks, only fifteen, than most of the manmade waterways it was still not a speedy way to travel, although it became more popular than travel by stagecoach as the number of those arriving in Preston steadily dwindled. In fact, the speed of a swift packet boat was barely 10 mph.

Nonetheless, the Packet Boat Company prospered with vessels running twice daily between Preston and Lancaster by the time of the Preston Guild of 1822. You could get on the boat at Preston at six o'clock in the morning and arrive at Lancaster for lunch having been served tea, coffee and other refreshments on your journey that had cost a couple of shillings.

A decade later, a faster service was introduced with iron hulled vessels more than 75 feet long and capable of carrying 120 passengers. These boats were pulled by two horses

The old Tram Bridge in 1864 showing the winding house.

Day trippers passing through Cottam *c.* 1910.

The once familiar narrow Aqueduct Street Bridge survived until 1964.

which were changed every four or five miles at suitable stabling points. Alas, the heyday of the canals was a short one with the advent of the railways, the Preston–Lancaster line opening in 1840. Nonetheless, since those days the canal has continued to play its part in local life as a haven for fishermen, pleasure cruisers and the wildlife which inhabits its length through the local countryside.

Unfortunately, the stretch of the canal from the bottom of Tulketh Brow through to the Preston terminus at the back of the Public Hall or Corn Exchange became something of an eyesore and was eventually drained in 1959. In its day, the canal ran up to town at the rear of the Harris College building in Corporation Street and this is recalled by local landmarks such as Kendal Street and the Lamb & Packet public house both named in reference to the days of the packet boats to Kendal. The Ship Inn, the Watering Trough, and the former site of the Boatman's Arms are landlocked these days, although they once served the canal travellers of the past.

Some five years later, the narrow aqueduct bridge that carried the canal over Aqueduct Street, which was a source of traffic congestion beneath, was demolished as that section of the canal was drained.

Back in 1887, the aqueduct that carried the canal hit the local headlines when an attempt to blow up the bridge was revealed. Early in the morning when a local man turned up for work at the nearby lime kilns, he spotted a length of iron pipe with a string attached up against the bridge. Fearing sabotage, the worker's foreman called the police and close investigation showed the cartridge was in fact filled with enough dynamite to blow up 80 tons of masonry. Clearly a lengthy fuse had been lit but the flame had expired, thus averting a local catastrophe. Had the plot been successful, the amount of water flooding from the canal would have caused havoc in such a densely populated area.

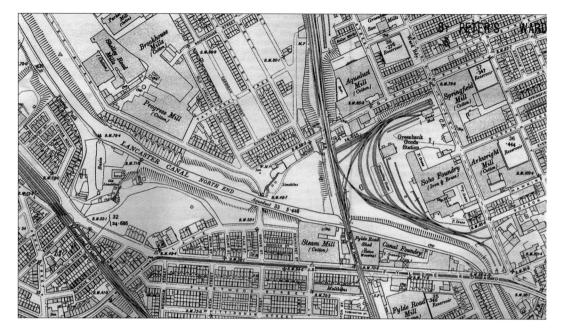

The route of the Lancaster Canal in the Fylde Road area *c.* 1909.

These days the canal is a great leisure amenity and over two centuries after the canal was opened we have the Ribble Link to give the canal system a new lease of life. Following the route of the Savick Brook, it provides a link between the Lancaster Canal and the Ribble Estuary and onwards to the Leeds–Liverpool Canal, via the River Douglas.

Spa Days A Plenty

There is no doubt that the Strand Road area of Preston has seen significant changes in recent years and consequently the names of some of the nearby places seem foreign to their present surroundings.

Back in the middle of the nineteenth century the area was developed to accommodate the buildings necessary for railway carriage manufacture. By the turn of the century the Dick Kerr works had been developed and tramcars were being built for customers worldwide. Spa Road is a reminder of the days when Spa Brow valley ran from Water Lane to Marsh Lane and there was an abundance of cool, clear, crystal springs. Alas the springs were confined to distant memory as the industrial development continued apace.

Spa Brow became famous locally for its open-air cold-water bath, which was constructed in 1708 and had adjoining apartments for dressing and a house for occupation by the caretaker. The popularity of the bath, which was square in shape with a flagged bottom, particularly in summer, saw it survive for over 150 years. There was a provision in the lease that stated the public were at liberty to wash and cleanse their skins for free at the stream of waste water running from the baths. Following the closure it was eventually covered over by heavy wooden sleepers, with several feet of earth on top.

It is believed that when Cold Bath Street was built, to the east of Spa Brow among the fields, it got its name through being on the route to the bath. This area was also home to Fish's cotton mill, known locally as Spa Mill because in the mill yard there was a long open spring in which watercress flourished. Bath Street at the lower end of Fylde Road is a reminder of the time when there were public slipper baths there that were eventually converted into dwelling houses. The only competition for the Spa Brow baths in the first half of the nineteenth century came from the warm and cold water baths situated next to Jackson's Cottage to the east of Avenham, but these were swept away during the construction of Avenham Park.

Water Lane appears to be so named due to the fact that up until the 1830s there was a well from which water was drawn and carted into town, selling at a half penny per can full. Wellfield Road owes its name to the time when green fields abounded in that area and a stream known as Spittal Syke served the well field there.

In Fishergate between Cannon Street and Guildhall Street there used to be a popular draw well, made by the Corporation in 1664. Three other wells to serve the town were

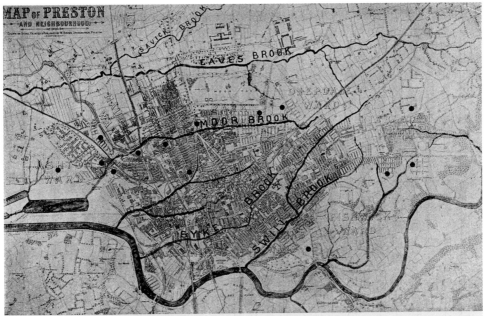

By permission of   Mr. W. Brown.

MAP OF PRESTON, SHOWING THE OLD WATERCOURSES.
The round black marks indicate the presence of sand pits used recently.

The old watercourses lay deep into the landscape in Victorian days.

situated in Molyneux Square, near the end of Main Sprit Weind and in Church Street near the junction with Manchester Road, which was in earlier times called Water Street. Many people in the Avenham district used to fetch their water from a well below the Avenham Colonnade, on the eastern slopes of Avenham, while along the River Ribble by the side of the Ashton quays there was a spring claimed to have great medicinal virtues. Of course, there was also the medieval holy well in the area now known as Ladywell Street, from which water was piped to the nearby friary at which place the monks quenched their thirst.

As long ago as 1729, an agreement was made between the Corporation and two locals Robert Abbat and Thomas Kellet to set works on foot to accommodate and supply the inhabitants of Preston with water. They took advantage of the several springs and sources of water and laid pipes down streets and lanes and preserved the existing wells and pumps. It included a cistern or reservoir down Glover Street and other resourceful gentleman joined the enterprise down the decades.

In 1832 the Preston Waterworks Company was formed and this eventually led to the mentioned wells and springs, and all the others, being drained away or covered, the Spa Well being the last to close. The company, keen to make their mark, made a reservoir at Grimsargh to greatly improve the water supply of the town, so essential for a place of manufacturing.

By 1853 reservoirs were in existence at Dilworth, Alston, Grimsargh and Fulwood; their combined capacity reported as 166 million gallons. In the next decade the Spade Mill reservoir near Longridge was constructed. All necessary when one considers that by the 1880s Preston required a daily supply of about three million gallons.

The reservoir at Longridge supplied Preston with plenty of water.

Inevitably, there remain many local street names that have connections with the streams of old origin like Moorbrook with its path through Deepdale on its way to Garstang Road, serving as it did many mill lodges en route. Brookfield Street, Brook Street, Moorbrook Street, Greenbank Street and Brookhouse Street are all reminders of the path of the brook which continued towards the canal aqueduct and on to the River Ribble via Watery Lane – that is until the river was diverted for the dock construction.

Then, of course, there was the Syke, an important tributary that flowed through Avenham, down the hill now known as Syke Hill and on to Syke Street where it fed the Avenham Mill reservoir prior to its passage under the gardens of Winckley Square, past the railway station and on to its meeting with the river at Broadgate. Then there is the Savick Brook that gave its name to the council estate at Lea with its Savick Avenue and Swill Brook with its source near to Waverley Park and feeding many a mill lodge on its way to emptying itself in the River Ribble near to the old Tram Bridge. Swill Brook Lane leading down from Frenchwood Avenue reminds us of a brook that was used by local women to do their washing as it flowed quite rapidly down to the river.

The River Ribble has influenced quite a number of street names; in the Broadgate area alone we have Ribbleside, River Crescent and River Parade besides Ribble Street, River Street and the old Ribblebank Street overlooking the river. Whilst the district of Ribbleton, not surprisingly, has a Ribbleton Lane, Ribbleton Avenue, Ribbleton Street, Ribbleton Place as well as a Ribbleton Hall Drive and Ribbleton Hall Crescent, reminders of the days of Ribbleton Hall, a bygone mansion.

The popularity of river names can be seen in the Ashton area with Calder Street, Clyde Street, Dart Street, Dee Street and Mersey Street all off Watery Lane along with

Rowing boats were a common sight on the River Ribble at Avenham c. 1910.

Tweed Street, Wyre Street and Hull Street. Besides these there are Tyne Street and Tay Street off Broadgate and Exe Street, Tees Street and Cam Street in the Deepdale area, Tiber Street and Arno Street in Frenchwood, Jordan Street off Fishergate, Tamar Street off Fishwick View, not forgetting Lune Street opened in 1802 and one of Preston's historic thoroughfares.

Then there are the street names influenced by the Lancaster Canal that in bygone days terminated close to the Corn Exchange. One of the canal wharf's tributaries was a stream with its source near Bow Lane in a field called Springfield, thus providing the name for Springfield Place and Spring Bank, along with Wharf Street, Fleet Street, Kendal Street and Aqueduct Street all which have links with the days of packet boats on that vital waterway.

So the days when the River Ribble was crystal clear and packed with salmon, when mill lodges were supplied by babbling brooks, springs quenched the traveller's thirst, cold baths were the order of the day, women washed the clothes in the passing stream and buckets of fresh water were drawn from the wells may have gone, but they are etched deep into the street names of our thoroughfares.

Going Underground the Best Way Forward

From time to time to make progress it is often necessary to go underground and such was the case in the early days of railway development in Preston. One legacy of those early Victorian days is the Miley Tunnel, part of the route of the Preston to Longridge railway. The railway opened in May 1840 when the Preston terminus was behind Stephenson's Terrace in Deepdale Road. Trains operating on the line brought the stone used for the construction of Fulwood Barracks and the training walls of the River Ribble to town.

Six years later the line was bought by the Fleetwood, Preston and West Riding Railway Company which constructed the tunnel running west under Preston, taking the line to Maudland. The section served by the Miley Tunnel was originally intended to be an open cutting. However, it was decided later to build a brick tunnel over it with the excavated earth dumped on top. The tunnel is in three sections, burrowing beneath North Road for about 400 yards, Moor Lane for a further 260 yards and below Adelphi Street for a 160-yard stretch. The gap between sections is short and as it bends along its way it gives the impression of being one long continuous tunnel.

The tunnel exit is just past Fylde Road and along from there was the Maudland Bridge railway station which opened in 1856. It was used for thirty years before the track

The Miley Tunnel entrance today – enter at your peril.

was connected to the main railway system into Preston Central station, thus allowing the Longridge trains to terminate there. The other end of the tunnel terminates after burrowing under St Paul's Road where the Victory Cinema, later known as the Rialto, stood from 1920 until its closure in 1958.

The track itself carries straight on from this point to Deepdale Road. At the far side of the road was Deepdale station, once a busy alighting point for local commuters including those wishing to walk up Deepdale Road to the football ground on match days.

In fact, both the Maudland and Deepdale stations were of an insignificant character, consisting of nothing more than a narrow platform and a wooden sentry-like box from which tickets were issued. In the early days of the Preston to Longridge railway, the carriages were drawn from Preston to the terminus at Longridge by horses. On the return journey, owing to the downward gradient, the carriages ran by their own momentum to Grimsargh station and were afterwards horse-drawn to Preston.

Steam power was first used on this track in June 1848 when a special train, hauled by the engine *Addison*, carried 150 passengers including directors of the railway company. The Deepdale station had its fair share of steam enthusiasts who would gather to watch the engines go past.

We must not forgot how precarious rail travel was in those early days of steam and accidents and incidents were commonplace. In April 1858 the first train of the day out of Longridge was less than a mile down the track when a local farmer, who was driving his cattle over the rails, was knocked down and killed. In May there was another fatality at Grimsargh station when a would-be passenger, who was worse for liquor, attempted to board the moving train and slipped beneath it to his death. The death toll of 1858 was increased on Christmas Day when a man who had been drinking in the Station Tavern wandered into the Miley Tunnel and was crushed to death by the 5.45 p.m. train, some 200 yards from Maudland station. In July 1859 a brakes man joined the list of fatalities, assigned to controlling the wagons from the quarry, he slipped between them and was crushed to death. Another brakes man suffered a similar fate weeks later at Maudland station while shunting a wagon into the sidings, being mangled to death between the buffers.

On a Saturday in August 1867 some 3,000 locals made the journey to the annual Longridge Guild celebrations. On the return journey one of the trains was delayed at Ribbleton station, and the following train crashed into it. Over seventy passengers were reported injured, although there were no fatalities. It was a violent collision with carriages wrecked, yet generally it was a case of cuts, bruises and sore heads.

Back in 1866, the station was the scene of a tragedy that would live long in the memory. On a December afternoon, a group of school children had gathered on the platform to await the passing of a train from Longridge. One of the group got her crinoline dress hooked on to a carriage door and she was twisted around ending up on the track. The following carriage ran over her and she died within minutes of being taken from the rails. Over the years her death has added to the mystery of the Miley Tunnel, a popular haunt for those seeking spooky thrills. Those with vivid imaginations will say that many a child has ventured into the dark tunnel and never emerged, while others will tell of hearing blood curdling screams echoing from the place on a dark winter's night.

In 1889 a private branch of the Longridge line was opened from Grimsargh to the new mental institution at Whittingham. It was built for transporting coal and stores

The hospital train ran until 1957 – pictured engine 357 – Riddlesdown.

to the hospital and it also provided a valuable service for staff and visitors alike. In fact, the hospital trains continued to run until 1957 and it was a sad occasion when the service ended. The Longridge line continued to provide a valuable service for transporting goods until its closure in 1967, the passenger service having ceased in 1930.

In April 1959 a LEP reporter made a trip to the railway and noted that the stations and sidings along the route were gradually becoming derelict. One exception though was the old Ribbleton station at Gamull Lane. William Glenister had been station master there for eighteen years and his widow Elsie still lived at the cottage. She remembered the days when the Ribbleton station regularly won prizes in railway garden competitions and loath to see the station become an eyesore, like Deepdale station, she was busy keeping the lawns trimmed, the paths weeded and the rockery well stocked with plants.

In later years the only traffic using the line was the coal trucks heading for Red Scar and the Courtaulds works. By 1972 it was the work of heavy throbbing diesels to make their way through the murky Miley Tunnel, through the signal-controlled level crossing on Skeffington Road and beneath the bridge at Gamull Lane.

The scene above the Miley Tunnel has changed somewhat since its excavation. Fylde Road did not exist, nor did the elaborate roundabout that it exits onto. And of course the canal that made its way past the tunnel exit is just a distant memory.

The Ribbleton station *c.* 1903 – it was known for its smart appearance.

The St Paul's Road entrance to the Miley Tunnel is nowadays fenced off.

A Red Scar on Our Landscape

Journey back in time eighty years and the area known as the Red Scar industrial estate on the outskirts of Preston, on the road towards Grimsargh, was a very different place. On a plateau surrounded by copper beech and giant oak trees stood Red Scar, a picturesque two-storey gabled building of timber and plaster. At that time in 1935 the land and property had just been bought from its owner, Miss Katherine Cross of London, by Messrs Courtaulds Ltd, who were busy erecting a huge factory in the neighbourhood.

This quaint, yet beautiful old mansion, situated in even more beautiful gardens, would always be cherished in the memories of those who have been privileged to see it, and will always be a source of interest to those who wallow in history. The plateau on which Red Scar stood overlooked the famous Horse Shoe bend of the River Ribble, and presented an enchanting prospect. Tall beech, ash and oak trees rose into the sky in all directions. In the grounds grew flowers in great profusion, and of an early summer evening the air was drenched with the scent of hawthorns, blossom and lilac.

The history books state that Red Scar was erected by William Cross, although a portion of the building was standing before the Cross family dwelt there. It is asserted that part of the structure dated from Elizabethan times, but few of its original features remained.

The manorial rights of this area were long invested in the Hoghton family, and were sold to William Cross of Preston. William was a wealthy lawyer who lived in a large house at the corner of Winckley Square and Winckley Street in Preston. His father, John Cross, was also a lawyer who owned much land in the Avenham area along with the Winckley family. William had often ridden his horse to Grimsargh and when he saw the great views he decided to purchase the run down cottage.

It was thus enlarged and altered in 1798, and again in 1840, when its library was added. A thatched one-storey wing at the north-east end, used as a dining room, preserved an ancient feature. This thatched wing was believed to have been a church originally. A large, blackened with age, carved oak table was believed to have been the altar and two old wooden candlesticks remained from early days. There was much evidence that part of it was simply a farmhouse in days past, with an old brew house, brick boiler, dairies, stables, and byres leading onto a cobbled courtyard. The interior of Red Scar contained much fine oak furniture, including a massive black oak court chest bearing the date 1368.

In 1813, aged forty-two, William Cross married and gave up his Winckley Square home to live at Red Scar. The family spent idyllic days there, walking through the woods to Elston and sailing across to Samlesbury. He never tired of the views of the land and the river from which Red Scar took its name following a number of landslides that unearthed red earth on the steep banking around the Horse Shoe bend. Incidentally, a landslide there as recently as 1950 swept away two anglers who were never seen again.

Red Scar – the much-loved home of the Cross family for generations.

When William was fifty-six years old he caught a chill and his doctor bled him – a common medical practice at the time – but William died, leaving six children. One of them was Richard Assheton Cross who was born at Red Scar, educated at Rugby, and later Trinity College, Cambridge. He had a remarkable political life representing Preston as a Conservative from 1857 to 1862, and in a second spell as an MP he defeated William Ewart Gladstone to gain the seat of South-West Lancashire. He was Home Secretary in the Disraeli government and later served under Lord Salisbury later. He later became Lord of the Privy Seal and was a trusted advisor to Queen Victoria.

Another son, Colonel William Assheton Cross, showed great courage in the Crimean War and later returned to Red Scar. It was he who had two observatories built at the mansion, equipped with powerful telescopes and instruments. The Colonel's son, also called William, later took over Red Scar and was the last of the Cross family to live there. The last Cross to own Red Scar was Miss Katherine, whose father had moved south to Devon in the 1890s.

After the Cross family moved out of Red Scar it was occupied by various families as tenants. One of them, named Charnley, was hit by tragic misfortune. A typhoid epidemic swept the area and Mrs. Charnley and her two children died from the disease. The last tenants of Red Scar mansion were Mr and Mrs Joseph Hollas and they often held garden parties there. The mansion was admired by all who visited and there was a hot house containing peaches, nectarines and grapes. The panelled dining room with stained glass windows was a particular delight as were the menagerie of farm yard and zoo animals kept by the Hollases. When they left in 1938 they chartered a special train to transport their animals to a new home down south.

Industry took over the Red Scar site from 1939.

Courtaulds showed no interest in the mansion that was left deserted. Eventually it fell into ruin – leaving only the remains of its brick foundations and the concrete bases of its observatory.

Just like the mansion, the great Courtaulds factory has left few visible secrets of its past in Preston, where employment was provided for so many. It had its own significant landmark in the shape of the two giant cooling towers once so familiar, standing over 350 feet tall. Courtaulds, who employed a great number of Commonwealth workers, with up to 4,000 employed at times, developed a massive complex on the Red Scar site. Vast spinning sheds and workshops filled the site as the manufacturing of new manmade fibres such as rayon increased.

The Preston site was not without its troubles with industrial disputes often to the fore. Nonetheless, the business kept many employed and it was a great shock to the town in November 1979 when Courtaulds announced the closure of the site with the loss of 2,800 jobs.

When the dust had settled the Central Lancashire Development Corporation moved in and bought the 250 acre site for £1.65 million. The hope was to create new jobs for old with the development of the Red Scar site into a modern industrial estate. Experts were called in to check for potential hazards left by the textile/chemical works amid the debris and derelict buildings. Much work had to be done, but the progress was highlighted in late March 1984 when traffic was halted on the nearby M6 motorway whilst the landmark towers were demolished. Two huge blasts signalled the collapse of the towers and traffic was flowing again on the motorway within minutes.

In the last thirty years the Red Scar site has developed into a most significant employer of local folk and there is barely a sign of the secret past of this corner of Preston, where William Cross rode on horseback to enjoy the tranquillity of the countryside.

A sign of the observatory remains today.

A landmark tower falls as Red Scar develops again into a hub of local industry.

When Secrecy Was Paramount

During the Second World War secrecy was paramount for security reasons with the saying 'careless talk costs lives' often heard. In that regard Preston was no exception and it was often, only years later that facts emerged.

For the town council, provision of air-raid shelters was a priority and they soon got things moving. Against the majority of large public buildings, whose stones were soot black with years of industrial toil, a bulging fungus of sand compressed into bags appeared. The familiar policemen had taken to themselves blue-black helmets of steel and carried a satchel containing a gas mask. On posts and pillars were fixed signs in red indicating to those in the streets where they might obtain shelter in the event of an air raid. In order to safeguard the public, the town council had spent considerable sums of money in buying sandbags, out of which they constructed substantial shelters; or they burrowed underneath the ground or created rows of trenches. With this in mind a town centre map was displayed showing the shelters either above ground, in a basement, or in a trench.

PUBLIC AIR-RAID SHELTERS IN PRESTON

Preparations against attack from the skies above Preston.

Certainly the Germans were not long in targeting the towns in Lancashire. After all, wartime equipment was being manufactured at sites such as Dick Kerr/English Electric works in Strand Road, at British Aerospace in Warton, at Salmlesbury and at the Leyland Motors plant in Lostock Hall. It was at Leyland Motors that 9,000 trucks and 3,000 tanks were produced along with millions of shells and incendiary bombs during the war years.

In September 1940 a German plane dropped explosive bombs at Fishwick Bottoms and on a house on Longridge Road, Grimsargh. Days later another plane flew over Preston, dropping incendiary bombs at various places in the town. They fell on a house in Derwentwater Place, on the nearby Park School, and on an army petrol dump in Moor Park. There were no casualties, but the warning was clear of the danger from the skies. Less fortunate were the residents of Lostock Hall in late October 1940 when a daylight enemy raid hit the Ward Street area with twenty-five people, including young children, losing their lives.

A few days earlier another lone German daylight raider had dropped two bombs and machine-gunned the Leyland Motors Farington works, killing three people and injuring over eighty others. Fortunately one massive bomb weighing over 1,000 lbs that landed on the tool room roof failed to explode and was defused by the Royal Engineers.

Halifax bomber cockpits and nose sections in the assembly shop on Strand Road *c.* 1942 – almost 3,000 of these aircraft were constructed around Preston.

In 1943 a captured German Messerschmitt was displayed on the Flag Market; in the background can be seen the brick-built air-raid shelters.

Years later, maps were discovered that showed the German targets around Preston that pinpointed fifty factories, seven bridges that crossed the River Ribble and public buildings like the railway station and the Preston Royal Infirmary. The biggest marked target though was the Preston Docks.

The Preston North End football ground was commandeered by the government as a prisoner of war camp for high ranking officers soon after the outbreak of war. The ground was guarded by troops and used as a short stay camp. The unfamiliar sight of barbed wire around the perimeter greeted local folk. Among the detainees there for a couple of days in 1941 was Otto Kretschmer, Nazi Germany's notorious U-boat skipper. He had become a national hero in Germany for sinking a record amount of Allied shipping.

Of course, Preston was not seen as such a risky place to live as a number of the big cities. The arrival of 4,000 evacuees – many of them school children – in early September 1939 from Manchester emphasised the point.

Throughout both world wars the Preston railway station was a very busy place, with many service men and women passing through daily. Consequently, the station's refreshment room was a welcoming place for food and drink supplied by an army of volunteers. Therefore in early July 1940 with the world at war once again there was much astonishment when two local men, one aged forty-eight, who lived in Brook Street and his nephew, aged twenty-two, who lived in Frank Street appeared at the Manchester Assizes accused of attempting to cause disaffection amongst soldiers who had visited the station's refreshment rooms. It was claimed they had spent an unusual amount of time at the station and the comments attributed to them suggested an intent to cause unrest amongst service men.

An army officer related that the older man had suggested to him that Adolf Hitler would not make a bad boss. It was claimed the two men had been supplying recruits with drink and attempting to undermine their loyalty to the cause. It was implied that their covert operations had been funded by a Fascist organisation bearing in mind their relatively meagre wages.

In their defence, the allegations were dismissed as unjust and without foundation and it was claimed that the two men had just engaged in idle chatter. However, the jury found both men guilty as charged and the uncle was sentenced to four years in prison, with his young nephew receiving a two-year term that Mr Justice Oliver felt justified his lesser part in what he described as a shameful affair. It was an example of the importance placed on secrecy and the fear of careless talk.

In May 1945 Field Marshall Gerd Van Rundstedt and other high ranking German officers were brought through Preston en route to a prisoner of war camp in the Lake District. When the train arrived at Preston, the buffet volunteers provided the military escort with cups of tea and sandwiches, but refused to offer the prisoners the same courtesy at a time when anti-German feelings were running high. Altogether 870 volunteers worked the buffet through the war years and every week up to 1,500 loaves, 1,000 pies and 6,000 cakes were devoured by hungry troops who were given mugs of tea and coffee galore.

A cup of cheer for servicemen at Preston railway station in 1940.

Where Secrets Are Revealed and Treasures Stored

Despite these days of recession the Harris Museum, Library and Art Gallery continues to progress in its endeavours to make it one of the top galleries in the country, much to the pleasure of Preston folk. It is a place that welcomes you with open arms, be you rich or poor, and affords you the opportunity to discover the treasures inside. The iconic building in the city square has been a great source of local pride ever since it was officially opened in late October 1893. At the opening of the building it was said that as the town's noblest and stateliest structure it would perpetuate the memory of the Harris family whose legacy had made it possible.

The opening ceremony was performed by the Earl and Countess of Derby, under the guidance of Alderman Edelston, the Mayor of the town, who had been a long time campaigner for a suitable free library. Of course, one of the dignitaries who felt the most pride on this occasion was Alderman James Hibbert who, as the architect of the building, had used the £122,000 share of the Harris trust, allocated to a free library, art gallery and museum, wisely.

Following the publishing of the will of Edmund Robert Harris in 1877 local architect James Hibbert was a popular choice to undertake the project, after all, fine examples of his work were already much admired in the town. He had been the architect of St Mary's Chapel in 1865, a building that cost £2,500 to construct, and had built a number of the fever wards at Preston Royal Infirmary, completed in 1876. Undoubtedly, the single piece of architecture that convinced all that James Hibbert was the man for the task was Fishergate Baptist church. This impressive Italian Romanesque structure that still graces Fishergate was constructed to the plans of Hibbert in 1858 at a cost of £5,000.

Alderman Hibbert chosen for the task.

Delighted with his selection, Hibbert was asked by the town council to tour Britain and the Continent to observe architectural designs, prior to submitting his plans for approval. It was a great honour for a man already a member of the town council and, indeed, an Alderman by that time. In fact, his work in helping to improve the standard of housing in Preston led to his appointment as Mayor of Preston in 1880. His mayoral duties performed and his plans for the Harris Museum formulated, he successfully gained council approval for a Greek Iconic style of building. Two years later, at the time of the Preston Guild, the foundation stone was laid by the Earl of Latham. What followed was a decade of construction and dedication to the task ending with the splendour of the day in October 1893.

In truth, the building was far from ready for the use by the general public who had to wait patiently until New Year's Day 1894 before the doors to the lending library, reading room and newsroom were opened. That day a steady stream of visitors, eager to borrow books from the new library, kept the staff busy and the reading room had barely an empty seat, with the ladies and gentlemen having half of the room each.

Looking after the library was William S. Bramwell, the borough's first public librarian, who was a familiar and respected figure in Preston, with his top hat and frock-tail coat. In an age of infectious diseases like smallpox, diphtheria and scarlet fever he had his own method of fumigating books that had been returned from an area where an infection had been reported. He had a special oven in which he placed the books for about fifteen minutes to sterilise them. He was happy to welcome folk of all classes into the library and he didn't mind the clattering of clogs through the building's marble hall. Of course, the library in his day had no electric lift and, despite his advancing years, he would gallop up the great flights of stairs with considerable ease. He only retired from his much loved post in 1916 at the age of eighty.

Alderman Hibbert was another with great enthusiasm for the place, but within a few years of the opening he resigned from the town council, feeling that his vision for the use of the building was not being realised. He had voiced his criticism in the council chamber and the local press and he spent the last few years of his life in voluntary exile in London, where he died in 1903.

Down the decades the Harris has acquired numerous sculptures and bronzes from the earliest Greek period onward, through the Renaissance to modern times. The art gallery was blessed by inheriting the magnificent collection of paintings owned by Richard Newsham. His bequest in 1884 contained numerous modern paintings, produced by the likes of Cox, Linnell, Prout, Creswick, Frith, Hunt and Landseer. The natural history department was soon to be admired also, with illustrations of animals and their habitat, and all you could wish to know about birds, both British and foreign.

A ceramics and glass gallery with an unrivalled collection of scent bottles was to become an attraction, together with a fine collection of porcelain and pottery, costumes and dress from down the ages which enthralled many, as did the decorative arts collection.

One inheritance that became housed in the library was the book collection of Dr Richard Shepherd, given to the town in 1761. By the middle of the twentieth century the books spread throughout the library were reckoned to number over 80,000 and the lending library had 200,000 books borrowed annually. Besides the books there are stored bound volumes of original local newspapers dating back to the early nineteenth century when the *Preston Chronicle, Preston Pilot, Preston Herald* and *Preston Guardian* appeared once or twice weekly, not forgetting copies of the *Lancashire Evening Post* from when it launched as a daily newspaper back in October 1886. So plenty to read within, and a chronicle of the life of Preston by the news reporters of old.

Additions were made to the art gallery collection on a regular basis and always created great interest and occasionally controversy, as in 1927 when the George Spencer Watson oil painting of a naked lady titled *Nude* was purchased by Sidney Paviere, just a year after his appointment as Curator and Arts Director. For 'adults only' was the cry from some quarters and led to a lively debate in the letters column of the *LEP*. In the post-war years Sidney Paviere visited many an exhibition to uncover paintings worthy of the Harris. In 1954 the painting *Chloe* – the child with the red balloon – by Miss Pandora Moore was purchased for 100gns and crowds flocked to see it.

Nude was a controversial purchase back in 1927, causing quite a stir.

Five years later Mr Paviere and his purchases were in the news again with two new pictures to display. Previously the record buy had been the £1,000 paid in 1944 for the much loved *Pauline In A Yellow Dress* by James Gunn. However, it was announced that for £2,000 a portrait in oils called *Dorelia* by Augustus E. John had been purchased – at today's prices that's the equivalent of £64,000. And for just £250 a controversial painting of the *Crucifixion* by Carol Wright had also been obtained. These days the annual Harris Open Art Exhibition, instigated by Paviere in his time, attracts hundreds of entries, reflecting the popularity of painting by local artists.

With an Egyptian Balcony Tour often available, a Foucault pendulum in tune with the rotation of the Earth hanging in the central foyer, a museum shop and the sweet aroma of freshly ground coffee, the place entices many a visitor.

The Harris Museum building is forever in the public eye and has had many illustrious visitors down the years, including Royalty. From the steps of the building the victorious Preston North End teams have looked down on the massed crowds in the Market Square, and many a politician or celebrity has acknowledged public support when paraded from its balcony.

Chloe was a delightful addition to the Harris Museum collection in 1954.

Once again in Preston Guild year 2012 it was a focal point for the thousands of visitors to the city, and it certainly did not disappoint with events and entertainment throughout the year. Last year a few eyebrows were raised when a flight of wooden steps was erected on the Market Square to give an unusual alternative method of entry for visitors. The 'Harris Flights' became the backdrop for a number of drama and entertainment events, including outdoor cinema productions that saw the steps used as cinema seating.

To the credit of the Preston City Council the Harris has developed with the times, with computers aplenty you can broaden your outlook, you can still browse the books at your leisure, you can view the many amazing paintings or artefacts displayed, or visit the latest exhibition within the museum walls. It has embraced the digital age and the contents of the building still astound us. Mind you, if Mr Bramwell was around these days he might want to put those mobile phones in his fumigating oven, thus preserving the sound of silence requested within the library in days of old.

It was built to quench the thirst for knowledge for generations of Preston folk and to that end it has served us well. On the Harris Road side just beneath the roof, inscribed in the stonework is the following phrase 'The Mental Riches You May Here Acquire Abide With You Always' – an honourable intention and one that has no doubt improved the lot of generations of local folk. Long may it continue.

'The Mental Riches You May Here Require Abide With You Always', words of wisdom inscribed in the stonework on Harris Street.

About The Author

Keith Johnson is Preston born and bred. His previous works include the best-selling *Chilling True Tales* series of books featuring Preston, Lancashire and London, and the popular *People of Old Preston, Preston Remembered, Preston Through Time* and *Preston In The 1960s* books. For over a decade he has contributed numerous feature articles on local history to the *Lancashire Evening Post,* and since 2011 has written a weekly Court Archive for the *LEP Retro* magazine.

Keith was educated at St Augustine's Boys' School in Preston prior to attending the Harris College where he gained his qualifications for a career in engineering – spending forty years working for the printing press manufacturer Goss.